Gil Stieglitz

Becoming
Courageous

Facing your Past &
Building your Future

Becoming Courageous: Facing your Past & Building your Future

© Gil Stieglitz 2013

Published by Principles to Live By, Roseville CA 95661

www.ptlb.com

Cover by John Chase

All Scripture verses are from the New American Standard Bible unless otherwise indicated.
New American Standard Bible: 1995 update.
1995 La Habra, CA: The Lockman Foundation.

ISBN 978-0-9838602-5-9
Christian Living

Printed in the United States of America

Dedication

This workbook is dedicated to Jenny Williamson and the wonderful work of Courage Worldwide in rescuing children from the horrors of human trafficking

Table of Contents

Introduction   7

Section 1: Your Past and Its Programming   11

    Personal History: Basic Questions   13

    Personal and Family History   19

    Getting Started with God's Wisdom   35

    The Nature of Spiritual Warfare   37

    Affirmations   43

    Warfare Prayer   45

Section 2: Closing Negative Spiritual Doorways and Opening Positive Ones 47

    Turning Pride into Humility   49

    Turning Rebellion into Appropriate Submission   77

    Turning Bitterness into Forgiveness   97

    Turning Lust into a Pure Heart   123

    Turning Anger into a Controlled Soul   143

    Turning Occult Practice into Worship of God Alone 165

    Turning Transference into Freedom   187

Conclusion   207

Introduction

Life is like a video game: we make choices and those choices make things happen. The choices that we made in the past decide what part of the game we are playing now. The exciting thing is that we can push reset and start the game over. We do not have to keep playing the game of life the way we always have. The fact that you are looking at this workbook says that you want to start seeing different results in your life – peace, love, joy, calm, self-control, deeper relationships. If you like the way your life is going right now, then this workbook is not for you. If you like the anger, the fighting, the shallow relationships, the hatred, the loneliness, the selling yourself cheaply, then keep going with what you are doing. God has allowed us to press the reset button. You can learn how to make different choices. You can behave differently. You can receive different results. You are not stuck having the life that you have had. You do need to change strategies. Ego and arrogance need to be replaced by teachability, self-awareness, and teamwork. If you have followed a strategy of bitterness, hatred, and vengeance, they need to be replaced by wisdom, forgiveness, and possibilities. If we have used anger as a weapon to get our way, then we cannot expect to have a calm and peaceful life. If we have used rebellion and defiance as a strategy, then we are eliminated from healthy, winning teams. If we have used magic, spells, curses, and rituals to try and control others, then we end up being controlled ourselves by the very forces we sought to use.

Jesus tells us the goal of life is relational. He tells us this in the two great commandments. "Thou shalt love the Lord your God with all your heart, soul, mind and strength. And your neighbor as yourself.." We were made to have a positive relationship with God, with ourselves, and with others. The healthier these relationships are the healthier and joyful our lives will be. We all want to have lots of loving relationships and enough time, energy, and resources to enjoy those relationships. Unfortunately our choices and what others have done to us has derailed us from the life we desire. Many have ended up in bondage to bitterness, pride, injustice, addictions, hatred, spiritual influences, anger, and other spiritual and emotional maladies. How do we get back on track?

This workbook is an intensive series of exercises designed to help you let go of negative patterns and embrace positive patterns in their place. This workbook is usually best done in a mentor-directed or serious small group setting. The answers from these spiritual workouts may surprise you. The benefit to your soul will be priceless. This workbook is all about life-change. If you really want to close any negative spiritual doorways that were opened in the past and move forward with positive spiritual power, then this is the workbook for you. This workbook is built on a Judeo-Christian understanding of the spiritual world. I am sure that there are other ways of understanding the spiritual world, but the freedom being pursued in this workbook is based upon a Judeo-Christian worldview and the Judeo-Christian God: Father, Son, and Holy Spirit.

Since ancient times certain activities have been known to bring greater bondage than others. These actions, attitudes, and emotional patterns need to be understood, confessed, and moved away from. They draw spiritual, emotional, mental, and sometimes physical bondage. These activities are Pride (Isaiah. 14:12-14),

Rebellion (1 Samuel 15:23), Bitterness (Matthew 6:12,14-15), Lust (Matthew. 5:27-30), Addictions (1 Corinthians 6:12), Anger (Ephesians 4:22-27), Occult Practices (Mark 12:29-31), Transference (Exodus 34:7b). Repeated involvement in these areas can block development of your life and open spiritual doorways where negative spiritual influences can begin to work in your life.

In each of the areas you will be given exercises to complete and room to write about your interaction in this area. This is a personal workbook designed to help you work through key spiritual areas. The process of change is between you and God, although it is often helpful to have a spiritual mentor work through this material with you. In each of these areas a suggested prayer will be given. This should be prayed out loud after you have spent time agreeing with God about that particular area.

As you work through the assignments in this workbook, you will be peeling off layers off negative spiritual, emotional, and mental influences from your life. With each new layer, deeper areas may be exposed which may need to be cleansed and released. This should not be thought of as quick, instantaneous, or hurried process. This is one part of the process the Bible calls sanctification. Throughout our Christian life God will be working on, in, and with us (Philippians. 1:6; 2:12-15). It will require work on your part to move into the freedom that is already yours in Christ Jesus.

Because we will be dealing with areas of sin that could connect to strong spiritual, emotional, and/or mental influences, it is best to begin and end every session with a prayer of protection and declaration of commitment to the Lord Jesus Christ. This prayer should include a complete surrender to the Lord Jesus Christ, an acknowledgment of Christ's complete payment for our sins on the Cross, the Holy Spirit's ongoing work in our lives, and our future place in heaven. It should ask for a complete block on the Devil's power and presence. It should turn the complete direction of this time over to the Lord Jesus Christ. It should include a period of time in which the wonder of God is worshipped for His essence, attributes, nature, law, and/or works. The following is a sample prayer of this sort.

Dear Heavenly Father,

I come in the name of the Lord Jesus Christ and ask for your protection and direction in this time. I surrender myself to the Lord Jesus Christ and acknowledge His complete payment for my sins on the cross. I yield to the Holy Spirit's ongoing work in my life. I am excited to know that God has a wonderful plan for my life, full of good works and joy (Ephesians 2:10). I am thrilled that I have a future place in heaven reserved for me because of Christ's death on my behalf. I ask you, Lord Jesus, for a complete block on the Devil's presence and power in this place and with me. I ask you, Lord Jesus, to direct and protect during my time on these exercises. I worship you, God, for you are all powerful, all knowing, present everywhere, and unchanging. I worship you, Heavenly Father, who sent His Son the Lord Jesus Christ to be our Savior and Lord.. I exalt you, God, because I realize you are Sovereign, True, Good, Gracious, Merciful, Loving, and Just. I am in awe of your work in Creation, Salvation, and the Scriptures. I look forward to becoming more like Christ as I cooperate with you in these exercises.

In the Name of the Lord Jesus Christ, Amen

All change is based upon two things: ***Adding something*** to your life that was not there before or ***removing something*** from your life that is there now. Since this workbook is about change there will be exercises that involve adding behaviors, thoughts, items and words that were not there before and removing some behaviors, thoughts, items and words that have been a part of your life. Be prepared to spend time on this process. It will take weeks or months as you uncover areas which need to be addressed. It is my experience that some people need to go through some of these exercises a few times before experiencing complete freedom. In each area there are multiple exercises so that more time can be spent in that area. Not all the exercises in an area need to be done to complete an area.

In order to move into freedom a person must do three things. 1). They must honestly agree with God regarding any sin or destructive behaviors they find in an area. 2). They must develop repentance plans and projects that will keep them from doing the sin again. 3). They must begin to practice a new way of acting, thinking and speaking to enjoy a different result. Again this process will take time. You did not bring the spiritual, emotional, mental, and physical influences into your life in a few minutes, so becoming free of them will not be done instantaneous either.

Information

In each of the areas, projects will be assigned that will ask you to list or uncover areas of potential sin and/or evil influence. Accurate information is essential to breaking each link of the chains that keep us from pursuing Christlikeness wholeheartedly. These worksheets will ask you to think about your life in ways you may never have been challenged to do before. In order to take advantage of the fullness of salvation and the freedom it brings requires exposing ourselves to the Lord's searching eye. This is not designed to be a morbid look at our past sins and failures but instead an opportunity to see if any of our past actions are still holding us back from fullness in Christ.

Confession

Some may not understand why a particular activity is destructive to their life or is considered sinful by God. If this is the case, then true confession and repentance cannot take place. Sin is always a form of selfishness that damages us, others, society as a whole, and/or God's reputation. It is sometimes important to understand the spiritual, mental, emotional, and even physical effects of a sin to truly agree with God that a particular sin is wrong. Confession can be done in a number of ways that is usually not effective. Some people only confess how bad they feel that they are experiencing the consequences of sin. Some are only sorry that they got caught. Some are willing to confess if confessing will free them from the bondage a particular sin has brought. Some may not truly understand how a particular sin blasphemes God or damages the fabric of their lives and the people around them. Until a person confesses an activity as wrong — regardless of whether there are temporal consequences — the confession is insincere. A suggested prayer of confession has been included that can be adapted to each of the particular types of sins that are discussed in this book. This suggested prayer allows for a full process of confession, repentance, renunciation, cleansing, and transfer. I have guided many people through this prayer. Even though it is long, its thoroughness in many cases is essential. At the very minimum, this type of prayer should be prayed over each category of sin, if not each individual type of sin.

Repentance

In order to take full advantage of the forgiveness of Christ and His grace, we must head in a new direction away from the old way we were living. This new direction is called repentance. Repentance means a change of mind, a change of direction. As you get started, you will not know all that is involved in how to build a positive, blessed life but you know that you want it. That desire for a new life in Christ is enough. The exercises in this book will allow you to bring the grace of God into your life in a way that you will start to move toward a new life. Realize that many of the ways that you have made your way through life are the reasons why you are stuck right now. It may have seemed like the way you acted was working, but it drove you into a dead end. God wants you to experience a new life path with new opportunities and new results. This means that you will need to learn to react differently and to think differently about how to solve the problems and opportunities of life.

Infusion of Truth

Jesus said that, "If my words abide in you then you will truly be disciples of mine and you shall know the truth and the truth shall make you free." It is not enough to just confess sin and work out a repentance plan that will lead you away from sin. Each person must have an ever increasing amount of truth transforming his/her mind. This process of allowing the truth to change the way we think is what the apostle talks about in Romans 12:2; Colossians 3:16; Ephesians 6:10-18. It is important to begin to examine and commit to memory the Christian's position in Christ. It is the truths of Scripture regarding our salvation that will provide our greatest hedge against the Enemy and the greatest hacksaws to liberate us from the chains of the past.

As you move through the exercises in this book, you become a spiritual explorer. I have included lots of different exercises in this book so that your exploration of your spiritual self will be more complete. The exercises were not meant to be done in order. You may start in chapter one or in chapter five. You may do one exercise from each chapter and then come back through each chapter for a more detailed examination of that aspect of your spiritual life. It is not easy to begin exploring your spiritual life. But it is essential. There are aspects of your spiritual life that are holding you back from life you really want to live and the life that God has planned for you. It has real areas of danger and deep mystery. Doing the clean-up work in your spiritual life has aspects of great joy and release. You are on the right track as you are seeking to clean up your spiritual world. The spiritual world can empower you to a whole new expression of the real you.

In Christ's Service

Gil Stieglitz

April 2013

Section 1

Your Past

and Its Programming

Personal History

Name:

Longest Residence:

Family: (Mom, Dad, Brothers, Sisters)

Extended Family: (Grandparents, Uncles, Aunts, Cousins)

Family Friends:

Personal Friends: (Past, Present)

Deeper Questions

These questions can be answered verbally or completed in written form to your mentor, therapist, or counselor. These questions are a part of the spiritual exploration of your life. You will learn many things about yourself as you answer these questions and discover patterns about your life. Enjoy the process. Usually it is best if you are writing down your answer that you use initials, a code, or some way of keeping the material secret from those who don't need to know this information.

1. What do you usually do when you get depressed?

2. When you want to have a "good time," what three things come to mind?

3. How do you respond when you don't get your way?

4. What do you do when you start feeling lonely?

5. If someone is mad at you, screaming, or yelling, what do you do?

6. When you feel attracted to another person romantically, what do you do?

7. When you have the chance to make a lot of money, what do you do?

8. Right after an argument, what do you usually do?

9. If someone has manipulated you, what do you feel like doing?

10. Who or What is the most important person or thing in your life?

11. When you don't know what to do – What do you do? Who do you ask?

12. What do you do when you run out of money?

13. What are three ways you earn money or have earned money?

14. Who are you trying to please the most?

15. What do you do when you like someone?

16. How would you let a person know that you are grateful to them?

Pressing Even Deeper

We must answer the following questions if we are to get a handle on what may be in the way of a joyful life. It is entirely possible that the following questions may need to be answered numerous times over the course of the sessions as the afflicted person opens up more and becomes more aware of themselves and their past.

1) What traumas, losses, wounds, difficulties, and hurts have I suffered through and how might they be affecting my life?

2) What is your family programming about how to deal with the problems and issues of life?

3) What is your current culture (friends, community, media, authorities) directing you to do, say, and think about the issues and problems of life?

4) What actions have you taken and/or words have you used that you are deeply ashamed of and wish that you could take back?

Personal and Family History

Most people learned the majority of their habits, systems, and ways of handling life from their parents or guardians. This next section helps you look at the habits and systems that your parents or guardians taught you that you may be unaware of.

1. Money

How did your parents handle money?

1.

2.

3.

What were your parent's sayings and attitudes toward money?

1.

2.

3.

What did your parents model in regards to making, managing, or giving money?

1.

2.

3.

Did your parents teach you anything about making, managing, or giving money?

1.

2.

3.

In what ways are you handling money the same way that your parents did?

1.

2.

3.

2. Success

What did your parents say or believe made a successful life?

1.

2.

3.

What messages did your parents give you about success in life?

1.

2.

3.

How did your parents try to become successful?

1.

2.

3.

What was your parent's success plan?

1.

2.

3.

3. Feelings

How did your family deal with feelings and/or expressed emotions; i.e. crying, shouting, screaming, anger, hatred, etc.?

1.

2.

3.

What did your parents say about people who expressed their feelings or emotions?

1.

2.

3.

How do you handle feelings? Is it like your parents?

1.

2.

3.

4. Roles of Men and Women

How did your parents model the roles for men and women?

1.

2.

3.

How would you like your mate to act?

1.

2.

3.

How close does your ideal mate conform to the actions of your parents?

1.

2.

3.

What did your parents model about how a man should behave?

1.

2.

3.

What did your parents model about how a woman should behave?

1.

2.

3.

5. Physical Affection

How physically affectionate were your parents?

1.

2.

3.

Did they say anything about public displays of affection?

1.

2.

3.

6. Compliments and Praise

When would you receive compliments or praise from your parents?

1.

2.

3.

What did your parents model to you about compliments or praise?

1.

2.

3.

What was the greatest compliment or praise you ever received from your parents?

1.

2.

3.

What do you believe is God's way of handling this area?

1.

2.

3.

7. Sexual Relations

How did your parents deal with sexual relations?

1.

2.

3.

What did they say or do to teach you about sexual relations?

1.

2.

3.

8. Loss and Grief

How did your family handle grief and significant loss?

1.

2.

3.

What did your parents say or teach you during times of significant loss?

1.

2.

3.

How long did your parents allow themselves or you to process significant loss?

1.

2.

3.

What do you believe is God's way of handling this area?

1.

2.

3.

9. Expressing Anger

How did your parents express anger?

1.

2.

3.

What did your parents do when someone was angry?

1.

2.

3.

What did your parents say or teach about anger?

1.

2.

3.

10. Parenting and Children

What did your parents do to train or control their children?

1.

2.

3.

What did your parents say about their role as parents or your role as children?

1.

2.

3.

What was communicated about having children?

    Joy, duty, drudgery, etc.

1.

2.

3.

11. God and Religion

What did your parents model about God and religion?

1.

2.

3.

What type of spiritual practices or religion did your parents practice?

1.

2.

3.

What did your parents teach or say about God and religion?

1.

2.

3.

What was confusing about their approach to God and religion?

1.

2.

3.

How involved were your parents in spiritual or religious practices?

1.

2.

3.

12. Conflict

How did your family deal with conflict?

1.

2.

3.

How was conflict resolved?

1.

2.

3.

What did your family do if someone remained in conflict?

1.

2.

3.

What do you believe is God's way of handling this area?

1.

2.

3.

13. Marriage and Singleness

What did your family say about being married or being single?

1.

2.

3.

How did your family treat married couples and single people?

1.

2.

3.

Was singleness an acceptable goal?

1.

2.

3.

Was marriage the ultimate goal?

1.

2.

3.

What do you believe is God's way of handling this area?

1.

2.

3.

14. Pleasure, Recreation, and Fun

What did your family do for fun?

1.

2.

3.

What did your family allow the individuals to do for fun?

1.

2.

3.

How much money and time was given to recreation or fun?

1.

2.

3.

What do you believe is God's way of handling this area?

1.

2.

3.

15. Race, Culture, Class

What did your family communicate about your race, culture, or class?

1.

2.

3.

What did your family communicate about others of a different race, culture, or class?

1.

2.

3.

16. Authorities and Power

What did your parents model in relation to authorities?

1.

2.

3.

What did your parents teach or say about authorities?

1.

2.

3.

How did your parents react to an authority stopping them from doing something?

1.

2.

3.

17. Politics

What was your parent's attitude toward politics?

1.

2.

3.

What did your parents say about politics?

1.

2.

3.

What were your parent's political views?

1.

2.

3.

One of the key things that these questions will reveal is that we have a significant amount of programming from our family, culture, or significant figures in our lives. The way they did things becomes the way we do things; whether their way was good, bad, or ineffective. The key question in this arena is: Are you learning, examining, and growing in wisdom to evaluate the best way to respond in the various circumstances of life. God has given us in the Scriptures -- His way of responding to life. It is His wisdom that will allow us to have a blessed life.

Getting Started with God's Wisdom

The Trade

God has offered to make one of the most lopsided trades of all time. In order to appreciate the trade that He offers, we must understand heaven's requirements. In order to earn your way into heaven, you need to be absolutely perfect (Matthew 5:48; Ezekiel 18:4).

Let us suppose that you are married and your spouse is absolutely perfect. When he/she arrives in heaven, the pearly gates swing wide. Your spouse enjoys the benefits and blessings of heaven as the result of living an absolutely perfect life.

Now let us also suppose that while your spouse is in heaven, he/she remembers you here on earth; and because he/she loves you so much, he/she wants you to experience heaven. He/she knows that you cannot earn your way into heaven because you are not perfect. So, he/she goes to God to propose a trade. He/she will trade all his/her perfection to you, and you will give him/her all your sin. God agrees as long as you agree.

So your spouse comes back and lets you know about this trade. They tell you about how wonderful heaven is and how much you would enjoy it. You agree to trade all your sin and wrong for perfection. Now when you approach the gates of heaven, they swing wide for you because you are now perfect.

The only problem is that there is still only one person in heaven. God loves the whole world and wants heaven to be available to the whole world (2 Peter 3:9). So, it cannot be just a man or a woman who lives a perfect life and gives it up for another. It must be God (whose life can never end) who became man, lived a perfect life, and then gave up His life. Then the trade can be offered to everyone. As many as are willing to trade their sins for Christ's perfection can be given entrance into heaven. A part of the trade is that Jesus Christ becomes our Lord and Master. In other words, there is a complete surrender to the One who was willing to take our sins. "He made Him who knew no sin to be sin on our behalf that we might become the righteousness of God" (2 Corinthians 5:21). "But to as many as received Him He gave them the right to be the children of God" (John 1:12).

Have you made the Trade?

The trade is made through prayer. Prayer is talking to God. A prayer to make the Trade would go something like this:

Dear Heavenly Father,

I realize that I am a sinner and not perfect enough to earn my way into heaven. I need your payment for my sins – the Lord Jesus Christ's death on the Cross. I right now want to make the trade with Christ. He takes all my sin, and I receive all His perfection. I realize that when I make this trade, it means that I want Jesus Christ to run my life. I also give you permission to make me the kind of person you want me to be. I thank you, Lord Jesus, for dying on the cross for me. I do want you to trade your perfection for my sin. I will let you be the boss of my life. Thank you.

Amen

There are two helpful ways to deal with the questions in this section. One is to write the answers to each question as completely as possible and evaluate if your typical response to the various scenarios mentioned here are the best way to respond. The second way is write your responses to these questions and talk about your responses with a counselor, close friend, or spiritual advisor. The idea is to understand your own personal history and how it influences your present choices, actions, and words. All of us are a complex cluster of systems, patterns, and habits that have brought us to the place where we are today. Much of the habits and patterns we follow we learned from others and have never really examined. Often this kind of evaluation can show where a new pattern can be substituted and a new very positive result can be obtained. It is not uncommon to need to write out our responses to these questions a few times over a period of time as we become clearer about our patterns.

The Nature of Spiritual Warfare and the Spiritual World

We live in both a physical world and a spiritual world. The physical world is full of elements (atoms, electrons, hydrogen, helium, lead, gold, tables, chairs, etc), creatures (insects, aardvarks, whales), beings (humans of all shapes and varieties), events (storms, earthquakes, droughts) and laws (gravity, aerodynamics, conservation of mass). The spiritual world is full of elements (love, joy, peace), creatures, beings (God, angels, human souls), events (creation, repentance, conversion), and laws (morality, redemption, justice, adoption). The spiritual world is invisible, generally, to our physical eyes; but we see its effects in the physical world. Every time we experience a positive relationship, we are feeling the spiritual world. Every time we see a good deed, we are viewing the effects of the spiritual world. Every time we see someone do the ethical thing rather than just the selfish thing, we feel the spiritual wind that comes from this action. On the other hand, every time we hear of a person being raped, abused, or enslaved, we feel the icy blast of an evil spiritual wind. Every time we experience injustice or hear of a serial killer's ways, we feel spiritual evil.

The physical world has both constructive laws and destructive laws which we would be wise to respect. We are constantly learning about how to utilize the physical world to construct a better life. The spiritual world also has constructive and destructive laws, and we need to pay attention. The elements of the spiritual world – love, joy, peace, patience, kindness, goodness, faithfulness, self-control, and the like – are designed to be used to build loving, lasting relationships between individuals, families, communities, and even nations.

In the physical world, the basic elements can be twisted, combined, and utilized in destructive ways. Unfortunately spiritual elements can be perverted and, therefore, weaponized to be destructive in all those relationships. When a person uses selfishness to twist love into hate or change energy into outbursts of anger, they have weaponized the spiritual elements of the world. Whenever selfishness gets a hold of basic spiritual resources and weaponizes them, this is called moral filth or immorality.

In the physical world if I leave damp clothing thrown in the corner and half-eaten sandwiches around, I will have a rodent, insect, and fungus problem in no time. If I do not keep my home, clothing, and living space clean, then I can count on insects, rodents, molds, and diseases increasing in my life. In much the same way if I do not keep my spiritual space clean, then I can count on spiritual insects, rodents, mold, and diseases increasing in my life.

In this book I approach the demonic spiritual world as an insect exterminator would a house that is infested with cockroaches, bugs, rodents, and mold. Demons are the cockroaches, insects, molds, and fungi of the spiritual world. They live off of the moral filth in the spiritual world they inhabit. We were made to construct healthy, loving relationships out of the spiritual elements that God has given us. Many do not do that and instead twist and weaponize the basic spiritual elements of love, joy, harmony, authority. This results in spiritual destruction, depression, and filth. This spiritual destruction, depression, and filth draw spiritual cockroaches. I understand intense spiritual warfare as an extermination model. The bugs need to be eradicated from the life of the person where they are present. Then that person needs to be trained on how to keep their life morally clean and how to construct healthy, loving relationships.

There are basic spiritual elements given to us by God in order to construct healthy, loving relationships. A spiritual periodic table of basic elements in the spiritual world includes: love, joy, peace, patience, kindness, goodness, gentleness, faithfulness, self-control, humility, gratefulness, curiosity, dependence, responsibility, grieving, righteous desire, mercy, grace, purity of thought, savoring life, harmony, boundaries (personal, familial, national). Any one of these basic spiritual elements can be perverted (weaponized) for selfish reasons. It is the result of the use of perverted spiritual elements that are moral filth. Their use creates destruction and depression and more immorality. Realize that what was designed for construction of a healthy, loving relationship has been twisted for use as a selfish weapon. It will damage the relationship and will like a half-eaten, discarded sandwich call for spiritual cockroaches. If a person has a demonic infestation of any level, then it is because there is moral filth at that place. The moral filth is either in the individual's life or in the physical place, family traditions, cultural routines, or other individuals that surround that individual. Wherever there is moral perversion, evil, hatred, and sin, spiritual insects, mold and rodents will gather to feed off of that moral excrement. You don't have to ask them to come. They will arrive. You don't have to bring them because they are everywhere waiting to do their work. Just as the molds, fungi, insects, and cockroaches will arrive when there is physical filth, so various kinds of demons will arrive when there is moral filth. They feed off of the selfishness, brokenness, and destruction that are in wickedness. This book is designed to help a person clean up their spiritual lives and begin constructing an orderly, healthy, loving life.

Love is the basic spiritual element of the spiritual world (like hydrogen in the physical world). This is why Jesus said that the two greatest commandments are Love God with all your heart, soul, mind, and strength and Love your neighbor as yourself. Construct healthy, loving relationships with God, with Others, and with Yourself. Every time I use one of these spiritual elements, I build something constructive in the world. Relationships are the most difficult constructs to create and maintain. There are thousands of things that want to destroy them. Relationships are the construction projects of the spiritual world. This is the point of being alive. Life is Relationships.

Cleaning out a person's life is one thing. Keeping it clean is another. Helping them construct healthy, loving relationships in their life is the third thing. Relationships are spiritual constructs. They don't exist physically; they exist spiritually. Healthy, loving relationships are made from the spiritual elements of love, joy, peace, patience, goodness, gentleness, faithfulness, self-control, and the many other elements mentioned in the Bible. We spiritually construct the relationships, and then we dwell within in those relational houses. These relational houses (spirituality, marriage, family, work, friends, church, community) are our life. Life is relationships.

By working through this book you are beginning a spiritual inventory of your life. You will find areas that need a thorough spring cleaning. You will discover areas where your present routines are inadequate to keep you free from spiritual insects, molds, and rodents. You will also learn some new exercises and routines that will help you construct healthier relationships with the people around you. I do have to warn you that not everyone around you wants you to be healthier. Some may try and resist the changes that you are making to your life. Some may move away from you because you no longer want to participate in the selfish and or evil actions of your past. Keep pressing forward, keep cleaning, and keep constructing your relationships in a healthy, loving way.

Drawing In and Embracing God's Wisdom in Christ

Exercise #1 Write out each of the statements and verses listed below by hand at least three separate times in a week. Live with these concepts and ideas and let your mind grapple with them. Ask questions and seek to understand what these ideas mean. God has some profound things to say to you about who you are and how much He loves you.

Exercise #2 Write down your observations about these verses. You may have dozens, even hundreds, of questions about these verses. Write them down and begin seeking answers to them by studying other passages, asking trusted mentors, and reading good books and commentaries.

Exercise #3 Write down the insights that come to you from reading and meditating on these verses. As you spend time in these verses, God will give you answers to various questions and problems you have had in the past. Let Him know that you are paying attention by writing down these insights, solutions, and answers. Talk about your new ideas with friends and trusted mentors to make sure you are on the right track with what you are contemplating.

I am God's child. John 1:12

Having believed in Jesus as God, He accepts me as His child.

I am Christ's friend. John 15:15

He calls me His friend because He is willing to reveal His plans to me.

I have been justified. Romans 5:1

I have been declared righteous through my faith in Christ's death on the Cross

I am united with the Lord, and 1 am one spirit with Him. 1 Corinthians 6:7

I have been bonded to Christ in a spiritual union which is indissoluble.

I have been bought with a price. 1 Corinthians 6:20

I have been purchased at very great cost to God, so God sees me as valuable.

I belong to God. 1 Corinthians 6:19,20

God claims ownership over me so that He can set me free to live abundantly.

I am a member of Christ's body. 1 Corinthians 12:27

God has incorporated me into the mystical body of Christ presently operative on earth.

I am a saint. Ephesians 1:1

Because of my trust in Christ, God sees me as holy and set apart for Him.

I have been adopted as God's child. Ephesians 1:5

I have been brought into the place of full privilege in God's family

I have direct access to God through the Holy Spirit. Ephesians 2:18

I can pray and know that my prayers get through because of the Holy Spirit.

I have been redeemed and forgiven of all my sins. Colossians 1:14

I have been bought out of the slave market of sin and released from the ultimate penalty of my sins.

I am complete in Christ. Colossians 2:10

I have all I need because I need Christ. He and I are a perfectly sufficient unit.

I am free forever from condemnation. Romans 8:1,2

God does not condemn me anymore because of my embrace of Christ.

I am assured that all things work together for good. Romans 8:28

God is so powerful and brings good out of all the evil that comes into my life.

I am free from any condemning charges against me. Romans 8:31

The Devil cannot bring an accusation against me that God will listen to.

I cannot be separated from the love of God. Romans 8:35

Nothing can separate me from the love of God that is Christ Jesus... NOTHING.

I have been established, anointed, and sealed by God. 2 Corinthians 1:21,22

God has planted me firmly to grow in Him. He has specially blessed me and marked me for heaven.

I am hidden with Christ in God. Colossians 3:3

> My real life is hidden with Christ, and all I really am in Christ will be fully displayed when Christ returns.

I am confident the good work that God has begun in me will be perfected. Philippians 1:6

> God has begun the process to make me like Christ, and He will not stop.

I am a citizen of heaven. Philippians 3:20

> My true home is in heaven with Christ. I am out of place down here.

I was not given a spirit of fear but of power, love, and a sound mind. 2 Timothy 1:7

> God has given me His Spirit to strengthen my spirit and give me new abilities.

I can find grace and mercy in time of need. Hebrews 4:16

> Every time I need God's power, His favor, His forgiveness, and encouragement, it is mine in Christ through prayer.

I am born of God and the Evil One cannot touch me. 1 John 5:18

> God gave birth to a new creature when I trusted Christ, and the Devil cannot touch that new creation.

I am the salt and light of the earth. Matthew 5:13,14

> God has called me to help preserve what is right and good in this world, as well as to show the glory of Christ and how life should really be lived.

I am a branch of the true vine, a channel of His life. John 15:1,5

> God has connected me to His inexhaustible storehouse of energy, creativity, and power. All I have to do is stay plugged in to God, and all I need for any assignment will be available to me.

I have been chosen and appointed to bear fruit. John 15:16

> God chose me to be one of His children. I did not get in by mistake. He wants me to show the fruit of the Spirit in my life.

I am a personal witness of Christ's. Acts 1:8

> God has empowered me to tell others what Christ has done for me.

I am God's temple. 1 Corinthians 6:19

God has established His eternal presence in my body.

I am a minister of reconciliation for God. 2 Corinthians 5:17

I have been asked by God to tell others that He is not holding their sins against them because Christ died for all their sins. They must accept Christ's payment.

I am God's co-worker. 1 Corinthians 3:9; 2 Corinthians 6:1

God has been willing to work with me to accomplish His will. He has, in some sense, restricted a part of His will to my cooperation. I am working with God.

I am seated with Christ in the heavenly realm. Ephesians 2:6

In terms of my position, Christ says that I carry the same authority that He has as the one seated at the right hand of the Father, the highest position of authority in the universe. Every other being is under that authority, including the Devil.

I am God's workmanship. Ephesians 2:10

God is working on me to bring me to completion and will not stop until He is completely satisfied and ready to enjoy eternity with me in heaven.

I may approach God with freedom and confidence. Ephesians 3:12

My ability to approach God is not dependent on my perfection but on Christ's finished work on the Cross. I have freedom and confidence in Christ to come to God.

I can do all things through Christ who strengthens me. Philippians 4:13

There is not a job that God will ever give me where He has not also supplied all the power I need to complete that job.

Prayers of Affirmation

Affirmations are spoken declarations of the truth or of your goals for the future. These are important in that they announce that you are appropriating the truths of Christianity or that you are headed to a new place in your life than the destinations of the past. There are two separate affirmations listed in this section. Try both at separate times and experience the difference the two different kinds of affirmations have on your soul.

Affirmation of God, Christ, and His Love for You

The first affirmation is about the truth of God's existence and His love for you. When you speak out what you are choosing to believe, you are sending a message of your faith and intent in the Christian life. Strong affirmations include the doctrines of God and the doctrines of salvation. The following is an example of a prayer of affirmation.

I recognize and affirm that there is one God almighty who has always been and always will be. He is one God eternally existing in three persons: Father, Son, and Holy Spirit. He is the Creator, sustainer, Lord of heaven and earth who is deserving of all honor, praise, and glory

I recognize and affirm that Jesus Christ is the Savior of the world. There is no other name under heaven by which a man can be saved. I believe that Christ came to break the power of the Devil and to set the captives free.

I recognize and affirm that God has demonstrated His love for me by sending His only begotten Son to die on the Cross in my place for my sins. I believe that Christ delivered me out of the kingdom of darkness and into the kingdom of light, and, I believe that I have redemption in His name.

I recognize and affirm the Bible to be the only written revelation of God's person and will to man. It is the truth of God, inspired, inerrant. It is alive and able to judge the thoughts and motives of my heart. I affirm that embracing the truths of the Bible will renew my mind and move me toward the goal of Christlikeness.

I believe that I am a child of God saved by His grace through my faith. This salvation has caused me to escape the wrath of God which will come, is presently bringing me into conformity to Christ, and will one day bring me to heaven to enjoy eternity with the Lord. I recognize that the gift of salvation is a work of God's grace; it is not a result of any work of mine.

I recognize and affirm that Christ wants me to be free as I abide in His words. I choose to understand the schemes of Satan so that I might avoid his desires and instead live a fruitful life in Christ.

I recognize and affirm that the Word of God is capable of transforming my life, and I present myself as a living sacrifice for the Lord Jesus Christ to do His will through me.

I recognize and affirm that the Lord Jesus Christ has all authority and power. I submit to the Lord Jesus Christ's direction and those things that please Him. I resist the Devil and ask that the presence of God the Father, God the Son, God the Holy Spirit, and the holy angels protect me so that I may glorify Christ. Amen.

Affirmation of the Blessed Life

The second affirmation is about the keys to a blessed and successful life as outlined by Jesus in Matthew 5:3-12. When you choose to declare that you are going after a different kind of success and a different kind of life, things begin to change. God says He can bless a life that is seeking relational wealth, not material wealth. He knows that it is only the life that knows how to develop real love and true wisdom that will ultimately succeed.

Read these statements out loud three times a day for a week and see new choices you are alerted to and what begins to happen in your life.

- I am humble, not needing to be the center of attention

- I am teachable, learning from everyone, learning everyday

- I focus on my God-given talents, gifts, and abilities, realizing I am not strong in everything

- I take responsibility for my mistakes, wrongs, and errors

- I grieve my losses: processing and embracing them

- I am flexible, not demanding my own way

- I remain calm when others are emotional and reactive

- I make positive, thoughtful requests and wise expressions of my expectations

- I act on my inner desire for the right, ethical, and God-honoring thing in each situation

- I quickly forgive people's mistakes, wrongs, and attacks

- My soul nurtures kind, good, and loving thoughts and plans

- My words, thoughts, and actions bring about harmony everywhere I go

- I am gladly willing to be insulted, wronged, and hated in order to stand with what is right

- I openly identify as a follow of Jesus Christ even if it brings insults and hatred

Prayer of Warfare

One of the things that can be very helpful as you press forward into spiritual freedom is to pray strongly for protection and power from God through Christ. These types of prayers are powerful ways to plead your case before God and gain new levels of His protection, direction, and provision.

Heavenly Father, I right now bow in the name of the Lord Jesus Christ and cover myself in His sacrificial death for me. I am thankful, Heavenly Father, that you have given me salvation through the Lord Jesus Christ and have given me the Holy Spirit to be my helper. I ask you, Heavenly Father, that you would protect me in the time of prayer and spiritual warfare. I realize that I am completely dependent on your strength, Lord Jesus. However, I know that your strength is adequate for any information or crisis I may face. I take my stand on the finished work of the Lord Jesus Christ on the Cross. As a believer in Christ I choose to use the authority that has been given to me to put the Devil and all demons under my feet as I sit at the right hand of the throne of God on high.

I ask you, Lord Jesus, to protect me during this time of prayer and spiritual warfare—to protect me mentally, emotionally, volitionally, spiritually, and physically. Protect my mind from all demonic confusion, logic, and fear. Cover my mind with the wonder and power of your salvation in all its parts: justification, sanctification, and glorification. Protect my emotions, Lord Jesus, from all attacks of the Enemy and bring peace and trust to this area of my life. Protect my will so that I might clearly be able to choose righteousness. Cover my will with your truth and peace so that I will not be tempted to choose impatiently or unrighteously. Protect me, Lord Jesus, in my spirit that I may be able to clearly enjoy communion with you. Keep the Enemy from attacking or disrupting this special relationship by flooding my spirit with your grace, insight, and mercy. Protect me physically from all attempts to distract away from you through my body. I ask you to cover me with your power and truth so that I would not be side tracked by my body in the pursuit of righteousness.

I ask that you, Lord Jesus, would bind any and all demons that may seek to be operative in or around me during this time. I ask that you would send your holy angels to fight for me and to minister to me at this time. I would ask, Lord Jesus, that you would cut off any assistance, any power, or help that may be given to demonic forces that are seeking to operate in or around me.

I ask, Lord Jesus, that you would fill me with your Holy Spirit so I may be discerning and wise in the process of liberating any way that Satan has me bound. I do, right now, surrender myself to the Lord Jesus Christ to run my life and direct me in the way I ought to go. I ask, Lord Jesus, that you would bring to mind those memories that I need to understand to move toward freedom. Do not allow the Enemy to throw images at me that are not a part of the movement toward liberty. I cover my mind with the salvation that is in Christ Jesus. I stand strong in the truth that Jesus Christ my Savior and my Lord is God almighty.

Thank you, Lord, for the strength of the weapons that you have given and may I become an effective warrior for you. In the Lord Jesus Christ I stand and ask for the fullest measure of God's grace. Amen

Section 2:

Facing Your Past

Building Your Future

Turning Pride into Humility

Isaiah 14: 12-14

Overcoming Pride and Moving to Humility — Isaiah 14: 12-14

Pride is a sin which destroys the future. Pride is an unhealthy self-focus. We are often unaware of the damage that pride does. The destructiveness of pride is the future that it takes away. All of us have opportunities that could become open new doors for us. We all have relationships that are just beginning or older ones that have the promise of something much deeper. Pride eliminates that positive future. In every case a positive future requires that we meet others needs, that we be others focused, that we get outside of ourselves. When we become consumed in a self-focused, arrogant way or a melancholy way, we are being proud and we severely damage our future. Yes, there is a place for self-examination, self-reflection, and self-congratulations; but lengthy self-focus begins to mold and rot our souls if we stay there too long.

Romans 12:3 tells us that we should think soberly and realistically about ourselves, neither too lofty nor too lowly. When someone you know is always bragging about themselves and their accomplishments, are you drawn to them or repulsed by them? When someone is always whining and complaining about themselves, their illnesses, their families, their relationships, their work, are you drawn to them? Pride destroys these people's future because the relationships and other opportunities they could have are never fully realized. Their unhealthy self-focus has caused people to move away from them.

The sin of pride was the beginning of Satan's evil ways. Lucifer was one of the most powerful angels (Ezekiel 28) and yet his self-focus caused him to want more praise, more authority, and more benefits. He, therefore, was unwilling to stay in the boundaries of God and began a rebellion against God Almighty. I can imagine Lucifer noticing all his wisdom, all the beauty of his apparel, and beginning to suppose that he should be allowed to do more, receive more, and be noticed more. Pride does not grow unless there are unhealthy times of self-focus. His pride destroyed his future in God's plan and twisted his legacy into one of destruction and imprisonment.

God has asked each of His servants to walk in humility. Humility means realizing that we have strengths, abilities, gifts, and desires that need to be developed and used for God and others. When we truly embrace who we are and develop ourselves maximally for the glory of God and others' benefit, we will have a great life. We must examine all the ways where unhealthy pride has spread through our lives and replace it with true humility.

A number of projects are listed in this chapter. Some are focused on uncovering pride and some are focused on developing aspects of humility. You do not need to do all the exercises in this section. Each week your mentor will assign one of these exercises and then pray with you following your work on that exercise. Then your mentor will evaluate which exercise would be the most beneficial for you to do. It may even be a repeat of the previous exercise. The large number of exercises are here so that lots of work can be done on pride and humility if it is needed and so that this book can be done over and over with new insights and new victories.

If you are doing this book by yourself, then do at least one exercise to uncover pride and one exercise on developing humility. Be sensitive to the Holy Spirit as to whether you should do more exercises from this chapter.

JOURNAL OF GRATEFULNESS

One of the greatest ways to fight pride is to become grateful at a new level. This exercise is designed to help you think through those people who have helped. This journal is designed to cause you to put specific events in their proper context, to give thanks to the people who have helped you, and to mention their unique contribution. Many times you will find that certain people are mentioned more than once. This is to be expected. They need to be thanked more than once. A heart full of gratefulness is a heart open to God's lessons and grace. Take each age grouping and think through the people who helped you in that time frame. Be specific with how they helped you. Make an effort to thank these people through a letter, a phone call, a note, face to face, etc., but develop a gratefulness perspective. "What do you have that you have not received?" And if you have received it, why do you act like you had not received it?" You may have to ask others about much of what took place between birth through age five.

Person	**Helpful Action**
0-5	
6-10	
11-20	
21-30	

Person	Helpful Action

31-40

41-50

51-60

61-70

71-80

      Once you have finished the assignment for your present age, regularly update the journal by keeping track of the people who are presently helping you. We need to constantly be reminded of the things that God and others do for us that allow us to enjoy the success we are enjoying.

Uncovering Types of Pride

The following is a list of the ideas connected to pride with their definition. Look at each of these words and write down any times you acted towards specific people in these ways. One of the most helpful ways to proceed on this is to look at the word and its definition and then ask God, in prayer, if there are any times you have done this to someone. Let God bring to mind the people and the occasions where this occurred. Don't try and invent these. If God doesn't bring anything to mind, then just move on to the next word.

Pride: inordinate self-esteem beyond one's achievements and merit; an unhealthy self-focus

Arrogance: an overbearing attitude of superiority

Bigotry: devotion to one's own opinions and prejudices without facts or before the facts.

Bragging: inflated or false statements about one's possessions, relationships, or achievements

Prejudice: a preconceived opinion about a person or group before facts have been assessed.

Criticism: the act of commenting unfavorably upon the work, life, person, or behavior of others

Haughty: openly and disdainfully self-focused, bragging beyond the accomplishment's worth

Unteachable: an unwillingness to be taught; a reaction to learning from certain people

Superiority: an exalted mental perspective about one's self.

Disgust: marked aversion and repulsion to specific people or groups

Hypochondria: extreme depression of mind or soul often centered on imaginary physical ailments

Melancholy: a depressive state of self-focus and irascibility

Depressive pride: A fixated focus on one's problems, difficulties, obstacles, and fears

Self-loathing pride: A fixation on mistakes, sins, problems, brokenness, victimization

A Prayer of Confession

This is a suggested prayer of confession. Take each person and/or situation where you have demonstrated an unhealthy self-focus and admit to God that you were wrong. This is not a magical formula; it is a suggested prayer. But the ideas of confession, repentance, renunciation, cleansing, and transfer are powerful. It is your sincerity and honesty before God that is important.

1. Confession and Repentance (1 John 1:9; 2 Timothy 2:24)

Lord Jesus, I agree with You that _____ is wrong. I turn away from it and ask that all the forgiveness that is in your death on Calvary be applied to my sin in this area. You say in your Word that _____ is wrong for you say _____. I realize that only in your power and through your direction can I successfully turn away from this sin.

2. Renunciation (2 Corinthians 4:4)

I repudiate, reject, and renounce any ground, place, or power I gave to Satan in my life through my involvement in _____. I give to the Lord Jesus Christ all power over this area of my life. I willingly surrender this area to the Lord Jesus Christ and the Holy Spirit.

3. Cleansing and Expulsion (1 John 1:9; Ephesians 4:27)

I cancel any contract I may have made with Satan through _____. I ask you, Lord Jesus, to cleanse me of any and all unrighteousness (including demons and demonic strongholds) because you say in your Word in 1 John 1:9 that "if we confess our sins He is faithful and just to forgive us our sins and to cleanse us of all unrighteousness."

4. Transfer of Ownership and Infusion of the Spirit of Truth (2 Corinthians 10:3-5; Colossians 1:27,28; Ephesians 5:18)

I right now transfer ownership of _____ in my life to the Lord Jesus Christ. I choose to take every thought regarding _____ captive to Christ (2 Corinthians 10:3-5) and allow Him full lordship in this area. I ask you, Lord Jesus, that you would fill this area of my life with the Holy Spirit of truth so that I would be wise, thankful, and able to see your plan in this area in the future. Thank you, Lord Jesus, for dying on the Cross for me. I choose to cooperate with you in _____ area of my life so that the process you began in me when I first trusted in You can continue. (Philippians 1:6). I realize that you want to display through me the character qualities of the Lord Jesus (Colossians 1:27,28; Galatians 2:20).

In the Name and for the Glory of the Lord Jesus Christ,

Amen

In order for a prayer of confession to be maximally effective in breaking very powerful satanic strongholds and influence, it is best if this prayer is prayed out loud with a mature Christian brother or sister who is watching you pray and is praying with and for you.

Exposing the Pride in My Life

This exercise is designed to take you through your life chronologically and expose incidents and issues of pride. Under each chronological period, make a list of significant people whom you have treated with any of these forms of pride. Again it may be helpful to pray before you do this exercise. *Dear Heavenly Father, I ask you to show me any ways that I have treated the people in my life with pride.* Let God bring people and situations to mind. Use the definitions of the last exercise to focus your thinking.

In what ways have I been self-focused in an unhealthy way during my **elementary school years**

In what ways have I been self-focused in an unhealthy way during my **teen years**

In what ways have I been self-focused in an unhealthy way during my **twenties**

In what ways have I been self-focused in an unhealthy way during my **thirties**

In what ways have I been self-focused in an unhealthy way during my **forties**

In what ways have I been self-focused in an unhealthy way during my **fifties**

In what ways have I been self-focused in an unhealthy way during my **sixties**

Looking at My Pride Through Others' Eyes

This exercise is designed to expose unhealthy self-focus in our relationships. It may uncover many of the same situations as the previous exercises, but it may help you see a way you have been treating people in a way that leaves you in bondage and your future unrealized. The following people received inferior, bigoted, arrogant, prejudiced, or haughty, moody, unhealthy cynical treatment from you at some point in your life. Please include a brief description of the episode or episodes.

Family Members:

Relatives:

Friends:

Neighbors:

At Work:

At Church:

At School:

Developing Humility

Humility means to know yourself and where God has placed you to make a difference. You are not the center of the universe but God does love you and has placed around you people, organizations, and institutions that have benefitted you and want to in the future. A part of humility means realizing that you have not and cannot fulfill your destiny without them. It is important to remember these people, organizations, and institutions with gratitude as evidence of God's blessing. It is also crucial that you thank these elements of God's love to you. It could have been an orphanage, a policeman, or police station; it could have been a government agency; it could have been a mission agency; it could have been a relief agency; it could have been a group of neighbors. The more grateful we are for the blessings and benefits we have received, the more seem to flow in our direction. Yes, sinful people and institution dysfunction and evil may have given less than was deserved or mixed it with evil but learn to look for the good. If we have a constant focus on the selfishness and evil in the world, we will become bitter, vengeful, and selfish ourselves.

Do the exercise by looking at people, organizations, or institutions who have benefitted you. The following people, organizations, or institutions helped me and/or deserve my gratitude and thanks.

Please note those who helped your and how you expressed your gratitude.

People, Organizations, Institutions	Expression
People: Family, Relatives, Friends, Strangers	
Organizations: Missions, Churches, Community	
Institutions: Government, Charities, Local, State, Federal	

Defeating Pride by Humble Service

Many times our self-focus has been allowed because we have not really seen the needs and problems of others. If we will offer to serve others with significant needs or those we have treated in a proud, boastful, or superior way, we can break the power of pride. Look at the list below and add your own service items. Ask your mentor about some other areas of service that would be good for you. The most important thing is to actually do a service project, not just to write down projects that would be good or fun to do. Go do one and enjoy.

Examples

a.   Volunteer in a special education or special needs environment.

b.   Volunteer to do the most menial job you can think of at home, church, work, or school.

c.   If your pride has been directed at a particular type or group of people, volunteer to specifically assist someone from that type or group.

d.   Personally apologize for actions, words, attitudes of pride, or arrogance to the offended people.

e.   **Offer to help those who could never help you.**

f.

g.

h.

i.

j.

k.

l.

m.

n.

o.

p.

q.

Developing HUMILITY

A good portion of humility is the willingness to realize that we need help or can receive instruction in all areas of our lives. In relation to God, we need a Savior. Without God providing a Savior, we do not have any hope of heaven. In every other area of life we also need help. Too many of us believe that we can survive on our own. But it is not true. We need other people. God has set up the world and life as a cooperative, team effort. Until we are willing to accept help, we will remain arrogant and proud. Pride eliminates many blessings because we refuse to ask or accept it when it is offered.

Follow the wise advice of those who have your best interest at heart

Take the advice that is repeated most often in the most categories and put it at the top of a list of self-improvement projects. Begin to follow the advice, counsel, or help if it is still applicable. Do the best you can at doing this new thing. You will get better over time. Keep track of the different reactions and benefits which come from this change.

What advice have you heard a number of times that you have ignored?

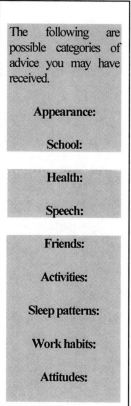

The following are possible categories of advice you may have received.

Appearance:

School:

Health:

Speech:

Friends:

Activities:

Sleep patterns:

Work habits:

Attitudes:

God has put around us the ideas, help, and direction we need to be saved from a multitude of problems. Begin the process of putting your life in a better position and follow the principle of salvation. Be willing to accept counsel and help. Slay the dragon of pride and arrogance.

Apologize for your rejection of wise advice and counsel in the past:

If you have offended people by your rejection of their sound advice you may need to go back and apologize for your attitude when they were trying to help. It is usually most helpful to do this after you have completed the next project.

Who has given you wise advice in the past and you have rejected it?

Friends

Neighbors

Police

Judges

Family

Counselors

Mentors

Relatives

Pastors

Teachers

Coaches

Drop them a note, phone them, thank God for them in prayer, write them a letter, send them a text or an email that says something like…

Dear _____,

I have come to realize how wise and insightful you have been to me in the past. Thank you for caring. I am beginning to listen now. Sorry I did not listen so well in the past. Please keep praying for me.

Sincerely

_____

THE CORE OF HUMILITY: SELF-ACCEPTANCE

Humility means knowing who you are and using your abilities, skills, and talents to help others. Self-acceptance is a key ingredient in true humility. A person must know who they are, who they are not, and thank God for both to truly have a firm grasp on humility. God has given you talents, abilities, temperaments, passions, dreams, and gifts that He wants you to develop and enjoy (Psalm 139:13-16). The following list of projects will move you towards the key quality of self acceptance. These projects are most helpful if they are done in order. It might also be helpful to find a more mature Christian with whom you can discuss your answers and pray. Self-acceptance is accepting how God has made you, realizing that He has made you unique, so that you might glorify Him in a way that no one else can.

Projects:

List the unchangeable characteristic about yourself that you would change if you had the power.

Physical:

Social:

Economic:

Parentage:

Ethnicity:

Temperament:

Heritage:

Learning to Serve

Ask God in prayer how He wants to use each of these unchangeable characteristics to give you the joy of serving. Write down next to each characteristic how that item could allow you to serve others.

Physical:

Social:

Economic:

Parentage:

Ethnicity:

Temperament:

Heritage:

Note: Many people reject or wander away from who God has made them because they can't see how that "limitation" will actually help them in the future. The true joy in life comes when you are being yourself: glorifying God, helping others, and winning for yourself. If our prime motivation is to be famous or use our success to obtain servants, it will result in misery. If our desire is to truly assist others and contribute to society and God's honor, then the Lord will fully cooperate in our efforts to overcome a limitation. God knows that the greatest happiness comes from voluntarily serving others. He places in our lives unchangeable limitations which keep us from being served and move us to serve others.

God's Ultimate Goal for Our Lives

In the introduction to the greatest sermon ever preached, Jesus described the qualities that are required to have true success. He said that there are eight qualities that are needed to truly be blessed. The problem is that none of us want these qualities. They do not seem like qualities that will propel us to a successful life. But God knows that they are the qualities that are essential to fully enjoying and, in many cases, achieving maximum success. Because God loves you, He has signed you up for courses in these eight qualities. He has arranged your life to give you the maximum possibility to develop these eight qualities. Many of your "limitations" are opportunities to develop one or more of these key qualities. If we can see how some unchangeable characteristic is designed to remind us to work on those qualities, then we can accept what God has done and thank Him for it.

Write beside the Beatitude the unchangeable characteristic that has or could potentially contribute to developing one of the beatitude. Also write down how God could be using this characteristic to develop one of the eight key qualities.

Humility:

Mourning:

Meekness:

Desire for Righteousness:

Mercy:

Purity of Heart:

Peacemaker:

Persecuted for Righteousness and for Christ:

Pray and specifically thank God for each characteristic which you have rejected but which you now see is designed for your ultimate benefit. Include in your prayer the Beatitude that you sense God is developing through this unchangeable characteristic.

Heavenly Father,

I come to you in the name of the Lord Jesus Christ my Savior, and I want to thank you specifically for _____. I freely admit that I have in the past rejected this part of your plan for me. I now choose to accept_____ and to see your plan for me because of it. I am excited about developing the beatitudes in my life. I believe that one of the things that you are doing with_____ is developing _____ in me, and I want to fully cooperate with what you are doing. Show me the ways that you want to use me through this "limitation" or how you want me to conquer this "limitation" and expand my life message for you. Show me new ways to view this area of my life. Show me new insights from the Scriptures about how you used this area in others' lives. Today marks a new beginning. I will let your strength become perfect in my weakness. Open my eyes. I choose to thank you for _____ and to receive this as a mark to remind me of your power, grace, and love to deal with anything.

In the name of the Lord Jesus Christ,

Amen

Positive Self-Acceptance

A part of accepting yourself is realizing that God has built many exciting talents, skills, abilities, gifts, temperaments and dreams in each of us. Only when we recognize these areas will we be able to accept ourselves and thank God for the whole of who we are. Make a list of twenty positive talents, gifts, abilities, and desires that God has placed in you.

Talents: A talent is an ability that you are able to do better than others. We all have talents. Some things are just easier for us than they are for others. The following are examples of some talents: singing, building, writing, speaking in public, telling jokes, making friends, listening, memorizing, analyzing, learning a language, organizing, planning, comforting, observing, drawing, playing an instrument, designing, color coordination, running fast, thinking quickly, etc.

1.

2.

3.

4.

5.

6.

7.

8.

9.

10.

11.

12.

13.

14.

15.

16.

17.

18.

19.

20.

Gifts: The Bible lists a number of spiritual gifts that God gives people that allow them to perform needed functions. God gives us these special abilities so that we will help others and so that we will have a purpose. The following is a partial list of these spiritual gifts: teaching, preaching, offering comfort, encouragement, leadership, organizing, making money, giving money, speaking praise in other languages, wisdom, collecting knowledge, seeing what God wants to do, praying for miracles, praying for healings, serving, seeing a need and meeting it.

1.

2.

3.

4.

5.

6.

7.

8.

9.

10.

11.

12.

13.

14.

15.

16.

17.

18.

19.

20.

Abilities: All of us have functions that we can do. These functions or tasks require that we be able to do some things well enough to accomplish that goal. We use abilities to accomplish these functions, tasks, or goals. We may not be especially good at them or we may be supremely good, but we often do realize how many different abilities we have and use every day or every month just to live our lives. The following is a partial list of abilities: read, write, talk, speak other languages, plan, smile, be friendly, use manners, plan, organize, direct others, comfort, walk, run, jump, file, type, discuss, critique, etc.

1.

2.

3.

4.

5.

6.

7.

8.

9.

10.

11.

12.

13.

14.

15.

16.

17.

18.

19.

20.

Dreams, desires, hopes: All of us have dreams of what we want the future to be like. Sometimes those dreams have been buried because of the problems of our life, but those dreams are still there. We need to bring those dreams out and examine them and start pushing towards the righteous ones. If you have righteous dreams that will bless you and help others and society, then you should pursue it. Sometimes you will find even a better dream as you start toward the one you have in your mind. What are the dreams that God has put in your heart? The following are some dreams: being a mom, living in the country, having a husband or wife who loves you, being a teacher, being a nurse, having a job that pays a certain amount per year, traveling, seeing a particular place, living in a different city, performing on stage, writing a book, helping people in a particular way.

1.

2.

3.

4.

5.

6.

7.

8.

9.

10.

11.

12.

13.

14.

15.

16.

17.

18.

19.

20.

Passions: All of us are passionate about some things that we want to see changed or that we really connect with for some reason. Those righteous passions tell us something about who God made us. Here are some righteous passions to give you some examples: oppression of women, orphans, violence, prisoners, church, family, marriage, injustice, preventing crime, punishing the guilty, drunk drivers, false teachers, false teaching, spiritual growth, exercise, nutrition, emotional health, after-school programs, fatherhood, healthy pregnancy, gangs, adoption, safe communities, guns, sports, reading, leadership development.

1.

2.

3.

4.

5.

6.

7.

8.

9.

10.

11.

12.

13.

14.

15.

16.

17.

18.

19.

20.

Please note that this list of positive aptitudes is one of the toughest areas for most people. Many are in bondage because they have never taken a solid look at the wonderful skills that God has given to them. Do not become discouraged that these lists take time. These lists will form the beginning of a completely new way to think about yourself. It will allow you to realize that God does have a plan for you.

Acceptance of God's Extended Training

Since humility involves realizing that we need further training, assistance, or correction, what are the activities, responsibilities, or talents in which you need help, training, or assistance? It is not possible to become everything God wants us to be by ourselves without help.

In what areas do I need to further training, information, or skill development?

Home

Work

School

Church

Dear Heavenly Father,

I thank you that you have died on the Cross for me and saved me from my sins. I am thankful that you were intimately involved in my birth. You placed all types of talents, gifts, abilities, and desires inside me. You have given them to me and you want me to use these aptitudes to glorify yourself, to advance your kingdom, and to produce fulfillment in my life. I will, allow you, Lord Jesus, to give me further training in _____ so that I might enjoy more of your love for me and the abundant life you had planned for me. By not using the talents, gifts, abilities, and desires that you gave me, I have only been robbing myself. I am deciding today to let you use all of me. I will cooperate with you to develop me into the full Christian that you desire. Thank you for making me the kind of person you did. Show me the ways that Satan has been covering the opportunities in my life. Allow me to see the new directions that will bring me into full use of the capabilities that you have put within me.

In the name of the Lord Jesus Christ,

Amen

Progress

Are you committed to progressing as an individual? God could have allowed us to be born fully developed, but He did not. Just as our physical bodies developed over time, so our abilities, dreams, talents, and gifts need to develop over time. Look what God says in Philippians 3:12 "Not that I have already obtained it, or have already become perfect, but I press on in order that I may lay hold of that for which also I was laid hold of by Christ Jesus. Brethren, I do not regard myself as having laid hold of it yet; but one thing I do; forgetting what lies behind and reaching forward to what lies ahead, I press on toward the goal for the prize of the upward call of God in Christ Jesus." Let me help you press on toward all that God has for you. The following questions are designed to help you see what God may want you to reach toward for His glory. It is important that you actually write out your responses to this exercise and begin refining your view of the future through prayer, counsel, and taking initial steps in these directions.

The future will unfold in amazing ways as you trust God and take steps in new directions to fulfill the righteous dreams He has placed in your heart. The future will not look exactly like what you can think about. In many cases it is better and it is always ahead of where you would be if you did not pursue these dreams through faith, prayer, and hard work.

If your life were perfect five years from now, what would it look like?

If God were to grant your righteous desires, what would five years from now look like?

Skills: Abilities, Talents, Gifts

Financially: Income, Savings, Spending Habits, Giving, etc.

Schooling: enrolled where, learning what, completed which degrees, trained to do what...

Spiritually: connection to God, connection to others, connection to self

Socially: Acquaintances, Casual Friends, Close Friends, Intimate Friends

Vocationally: What are you doing, Where do you work, Promotions, Pay,

Emotionally: Ability to express, ability to feel, control over emotions, fears faced...

Physically: Health and fitness

Mentally: Thoughts, Attitudes, Plans

Turning Rebellion

into

Appropriate Submission

1 Samuel 15:23; 1 Peter 2:13

Turning Rebellion into Appropriate Submission 1 Samuel 15:23; 1 Peter 2:13

One of the key areas which the Devil can gain a foothold in our life is rebellion and the unwillingness to submit to God-given authorities. When people are unwilling to take direction from authority, they are unable to take direction from God. Their rebellion often leaves them vulnerable to greater temptation and robs them of being in the center of God's will. While some carry rebellion to an unhealthy extreme, most people are guilty of some level of selfish rebellion. In this chapter there are a number of exercises that will help you develop a healthy relationship with authority. You may not need to do all the exercises in this chapter but only a few. Allow your mentor to work with you on various exercises to make progress in this area of appropriate relationships with authority

Rebellion is refusing to adapt myself to the needs, desires, and direction of my God-given authorities.

God has placed in our lives authorities to protect us, bless us, direct us, provide for us, and, at times, to focus us through limits. These God-given authorities are not perfect but are in place to channel God's grace to us. These God-given authorities are: parents, government officials, church leaders, employers, mates, and God Himself. When we rebel from these authorities needlessly, we miss God's best for us. Yes, there may be times when we need to rebel from these authorities because what they are asking us to do is evil in some form. Rebellion in refusing to participate in evil is not wrong, but it is about selfish control of our lives.

Make a list of the God-given authorities you have rebelled against needlessly by ignoring, deflecting, or refusing to do what they asked, directed, or commanded. Also list in general terms the nature of the rebellion. Please list those you have rebelled against in each category and include specific areas of rebellion.

People	Rebellion

Parents:

Government officials:

Employers:

Spouse:

Church Leaders:

God:

Confession

This is the time to agree with God that certain times of rebellion in your life have been wrong. This is a suggested prayer of confession. You do not have to use these exact words, but these ideas of confession, repentance, renunciation, cleansing, and transfer should be present. This is not a magical formula; it is a suggested prayer. It is your sincerity and honesty before God that is important.

1. Confession and Repentance (1 John 1:9; 2 Timothy 2:24)

*Lord Jesus, I agree with You that _____ is wrong. I turn **away** from it and ask that all the forgiveness that is in your death on Calvary be applied to my sin in this area. You say in your Word that _____ is wrong for you say _____. I realize that only in your power and energy and through your direction can I successfully turn away from this sin.*

2. Renunciation (2 Corinthians 4:4)

I repudiate, reject, and renounce any ground, place, or power I gave to Satan in my life through my involvement in _____. I give to the Lord Jesus Christ all power over this area of my life. I willingly surrender this area to the Lord Jesus Christ and the Holy Spirit.

3. Cleansing and Expulsion (1 John 1:9; Ephesians 4:27)

I cancel any contract I may have made with Satan through _____. I ask you, Lord Jesus, to cleanse me of any and all unrighteousness (including demons and demonic strongholds) because you say in your Word in 1 John 1:9 that "if we confess our sins He is faithful and just to forgive us our sins and to cleanse us of all unrighteousness."

4. Transfer of Ownership and Infusion of the Spirit of Truth (2 Corinthians 10:3-5; Colossians 1:27,28; Ephesians 5:18)

I right now transfer ownership of _____ in my life to the Lord Jesus Christ. I choose to take every thought regarding _____ captive to Christ (2 Corinthians 10:3-5) and allow Him full lordship in this area. I ask you, Lord Jesus, that you would fill this area of my life with the Holy Spirit of truth so that I would be wise, thankful, and able to see your plan in this area in the future. Thank you, Lord Jesus, for dying on the Cross for me. I choose to cooperate with you in _____ area of my life so that the process you began in me when I first trusted in you can continue. (Philippians 1:6) I realize that you want to display through me the character qualities of the Lord Jesus (Colossians 1:27,28; Galatians 2:20).

In the Name and for the Glory of the Lord Jesus Christ,

Amen

In order for a prayer of confession to be maximally effective in breaking very powerful satanic strongholds and influence, it is best if this prayer is prayed out loud with a mature Christian brother or sister who is praying with and for you.

APPROPRIATE SUBMISSION is willingly adapting myself to the needs, desires, and commands of God-given authority. There are five major blessings or benefits which God provides for developing the quality of submission. As we discuss each of the blessings of submission, we will assign a project(s) to develop this aspect of adaptation (submission) in your life, protection, provision, direction, refinement, appeal.

The first major blessing that comes from righteous submission is Protection: By responding willingly to our authorities' commands, needs, and desires, we are removed from the temptations and influences designed to destroy us (1 Samuel 15:23). We are protected from many of the difficulties that surround us in the world. Yes, we are allowed to resist commands that are evil, immoral, or unethical but those are usually rare.

When we rebel from a God-given authority, we are immediately exposed to a greater level of satanic attack – usually in the form of a temptation (1 Samuel 15:23). My rebellion exposes me to a stronger level of temptation in particular areas than if I were to have a healthy relationship with my authorities. One man explained that he tried an experiment where he would purposely rebel (or resist) the direction of an authority to see what the temptation would be. He was amazed that when he openly rebelled the direction of his boss at work, he had an almost instant desire to get drunk and chase women. When he told his boss that he was wrong for his defiance, the temptation died down.

Look over this list of sins and see if you are more tempted to do these after you have rebelled. Are any of your sins connected to rebellion? "When I rebel from my authorities I am temptations to…."

Authority	**Temptation**	
		Arrogance, prejudice, bigotry, pornography, adultery, change religions, homosexuality, anger, gossip, slander, overeating, drunkenness, smoking, drug abuse, self-abuse, stealing, hatred, lying, false religions or false worship, self-pity, depression, suicide, laziness, wrong friends, cussing or swearing, blasphemy, bitterness, strife, gossip, violence, vengeance, immorality, fraud, etc.
Parents:		
Government officials:		
Employers:		
Spouse:		
Church leaders:		
God:		

If you were to do exactly what your authority wanted in each area, what would you no longer be doing?

1.

2.

3.

4.

5.

The second major blessing which comes with righteous submission is Provision: Each God-given authority supplies crucial provisions (spiritual, mental, emotional, physical, relational, financial) to meet specific needs in our lives (Romans 13:1-8). If an authority does not provide the basic provisions that God has assigned, then it forfeits the right to rule in our lives. Make a list of the provisions that each authority provides (or should) provide in your life.

God:

Church Leaders:

Government:

Parents:

Spouse:

Employer:

Missing Provisions: What provisions have you missed or lacked in the past because of your rebellion? Please write down any specific provisions that you think of or God brings to your mind that might have been yours without your rebellion.

Spiritual

Mental

Emotional

Physical

Relational

Financial

The third major blessing that comes from righteous submission is Direction: God communicates major parts of His specific plan for us through our authorities. Therefore by willingly adapting to our authorities, we can discern the will of God (1 Peter 2:13-15).

Sometimes we think we know what our authorities want, but we have not asked or have misunderstood what they really want. After you have answered these questions to the best of your ability, ask them what they want you to do. You may be surprised at what your authority really wants. One of the greatest rebukes to a rebellious heart is to ask your God-given authorities about what they really want you to do. Let them know that you are willing to submit to their righteous requests. The following exercise is designed to bring your righteous submission into the open where it can be seen, exercised, and challenged.

Check the appropriate item when it has been completed for each authority

Parents

- o I have a list of expectations of my parents in order to please them.

- o I have let them know that I believe that God will be guiding me through their decisions within God-given guidelines.

- o I have asked for their forgiveness for my rebellious actions, attitudes, and words in the past.

Government officials

- o I have a list of expectations of the federal, state, and local governments in order to please them.

- o I have let them know that I believe that God will be guiding me through their decisions within God-given guidelines.

- o I have asked for their forgiveness for my rebellious actions, attitudes, and words in the past.

Employers

- o I have a list of expectations of my bosses in order to please them.

- o I have let them know that I believe that God will be guiding me through their decisions within God-given guidelines.

- o I have asked for their forgiveness for my rebellious actions, attitudes, and words in the past.

Spouse

- o   I have a list of expectations of my spouse in order to please him/her.

- o   I have let him/her know that I believe that God will be guiding me through his/her decisions within God-given guidelines.

- o   I have asked for his/her forgiveness for my rebellious actions, attitudes, and words in the past.

God

- o   I have a list of expectations of God's in order to please Him.

- o   I have let Him know that I believe that He will be guiding me through prompting and Scripture reading.

- o   I have asked Him for forgiveness for my rebellious actions, attitudes, and words in the past.

Undoing Rebellion and Beginning Appropriate Submission

If you were doing what you're God-given authority righteously directed and even wished, what would that be? We often have never really sat down and wrote down what our authorities want. We just know that we have something else in mind whenever they ask for something. Write down what you think they want you to do. Then look at the list. Cross off anything that is immoral, illegal or unethical. Picture yourself actually doing what is left on the list. What comes to your mind when you picture yourself actually doing what your righteous authority wants. This is not about doing anything immoral, illegal, or unethical that any authority may want. It is about learning to have a healthy relationship with your authorities.

Parents:

Government Officials:

Employers:

Spouse:

Church Leaders:

God:

Gaining clear direction: Make a list of your proposed actions and goals for the coming week and submit this to your authority for review. They can change, add, delete, and rearrange. Use the following categories to spur your goals.

Personal

Relationships

Family

Church

Purchases

Work

Phone

Finances

If I were to ask your authorities, would they say that you tend to resist their direction or that you willingly adjust to their direction, needs, and desires?

God

Church Leaders

Government

Parents

Spouse

Employers

Insight into missing God's will: Can you see specific places where you may have missed God's best by rebelling from your God-given authorities? If yes, please cite the instance.

Spirituality

Personal Development

Marriage/Dating

Family

Work

Church

Finances

Friends

Society

Enemies

Let your authorities know that you realize that God is going to be directing you through them (as long as it is not illegal, immoral, or illicit). Also ask them for direction regarding a specific question you have regarding God's will (make sure it relates to their responsibilities).

The fourth major blessing that comes from righteous submission is Refinement: God places each of us in specific authority-submission relationships to chip and polish off the rough spots in our lives so that we can become all God intends for us (Ephesians 5:25-26). The following was written by Charlie "Tremendous" Jones. "The person who is not learning about discipline by subjecting himself to authority can try all the self-disciplining he wants, but he'll never be successful. He has no discipline to apply discipline. Many people fail because they fail to exercise this essential quality."

What is God trying to work on in your life through each authority?

God is more interested in your having an abundant life (John 10:10) than you are. He wants you to enjoy the wonders of love, joy, peace, patience, kindness, goodness, gentleness, faithfulness, and self-control even within the context you are presently living. He wants to change your life by changing you on the inside. Therefore God is working on you to move you forward to a great life. He signs you up for courses in the key qualities that are needed for a great life. When you develop the qualities, you pass the course and God can move on to the next quality. If you don't pass the course because you refuse to develop the quality – because you are blaming everyone, criticizing, refusing to look for the good, refusing to see the opportunity or shrink back from growth – then the course repeats. God is trying to bless you by some of the difficult things in your life. He does not cause the evil, but He can even use the evil to refine us into great people. What is God's curriculum chart? Look at the Beatitudes (Matthew 5:3-12) and the Fruit of the Spirit (Galatians 5:22,23). God knows you will not have the life you really want without these qualities so He is enrolling you in these courses. What God might be working on with one authority may be completely different than what He is working on with other authorities. The key is to cooperate with what God is doing so that you can attain that next step of love, blessing, and encouragement.

God

Church Leaders

Government

Parents:

Spouse

Employer

Humility
Teachable, Acceptance, Gratefulness
Mourning
Responsibility, Processing loss and pain, Confession of Sin
Meekness
Anger managements, yield rights
Desire for Righteousness
Passion, cause, dream
Mercy
Commitment to Relationship, Forgiveness, Release vengeance
Purity of Heart
Positive Mental World, Love not Lust,
Peacemaker
Savoring life, At peace, making peace
Persecuted for Right & Christ
Moral Boundaries, Moral Actions, Open Commitment to Christ

What quality or ability needs to be changed or developed in you that will most likely not be developed except through the pressure of an authority?

It may be different under each authority.

God

Church Leaders

Government

Parents

Spouse

Employer

Love
Joy
Peace
Patience
Kindness
Goodness
Gentleness
Faithfulness
Self-Control

What positive work has God done in the past through your authorities?

It is often so easy to only look at where our authorities failed instead of looking at where they succeed. We don't want to minimize where our authorities were evil, illegal, or unethical; but we need to look hard at what they did right. Where did your authorities cooperate with God and provide you with protection, provision, direction, refinement, and appeal? We need to be grateful for these powerful evidences of God's love for us. Yes, your authorities were not perfect but they did some things well. We have often fixated on their failings that we cannot see their successes.

God

Church Leaders

Protection
Provision
Direction
Refinement
Appeal

Government

Parents

Spouse

Employer

The fifth major blessing that comes from righteous submission is Appeal: Only through a willingly adapting to my God-given authority am I in a place to correct, redirect, cancel, or adjust a specific decision or direction (1 Peter 3:1-6; 1 Samuel 25). We must realize that authorities listen to those who have demonstrated a team player point of view in the past. Authorities want to see a willingness to sacrifice for the good of the team. The malcontent is usually turned off. The person who is always complaining is ignored after awhile. The person who is negative about every new initiative and direction becomes an irritating noise rather than a trusted advisor. Just because you can see all the things that are wrong with an operation does not mean that the changes will be made.

What direction that an authority is suggesting seems to need to change or is wrong?

God

Church Leaders

Government

Parents

Spouse

Employer

What is the basic intent of the inappropriate direction or decision?

You must understand the intention of the authority before you can make an appeal. The authority has an opinion that what they are seeking to do will accomplish what they intent. If you can clearly demonstrate that your authorities intent will not be accomplished by their directive or program, then you have a basis for an appeal.

God

Church Leaders

Government

Parents

Spouse

Employer

Rehearse your wording so that your appeal is well received.

An appeal must be positive. It must rehearse their past success. It must be stated in terms of their perspective – why they would want this change. It must refer to their intent not just your ideas or goals. An appeal must leave the final decision in their hands. This type of appeal usually is heard and often causes changes.

The Dangers of Over-Submission

If we fail to develop the quality of submission and chose to rebel, we miss out on all the above blessings: protection, provision, direction, refinement, appeal. But don't go too far in your submission. A person should not submit to doing evil. A person should not devalue or degrade their own personhood through submission. Submission is an essential action to develop true greatness. Submission is adaptation. Submission is team play. Submission is role differentiation. Submission is recognizing responsibility. Without submission, everyone is on their own and the tyranny of individual power runs rampant. Therefore submission is required for every organization, every institution, every church, every business, every marriage, every family, and every person. Remember we do not adapt out of fear but because God has asked us to demonstrate His glory and receive His blessing this way. But there is a danger in submission: being forced to submit or submitting our personhood and value to oppression by the other person.

God has given us in the Ten Commandments the boundaries of submission. He has asked us to behave in these ways, but He has also given us the way that people should treat us. We must not allow, if it is at all possible, for others to treat us in the following abusive ways. I have my children say the Ten Commandments every day and now I also have them say these boundaries for how others should treat them. I have actually made the following lists into placemats for the dinner table so that we all see these issues all the time.

The  Commandments

You shall have no other god's before Me

You shall not make for yourselves any graven images

You shall not take the Name of the Lord your God in vain

Remember the Sabbath day to keep it holy

Honor your Father and your Mother

You shall not murder

You shall not commit adultery

You shall not steal

You shall not bear false witness against your neighbor

You shall not covet anything that belongs to your neighbor

1. I will not allow myself to be spiritually abused or manipulated

No god but God; no spiritual authority has the right to violate these boundaries

2. I will not allow God to be misrepresented to me

No distortions of the God of the Bible

3. I will not allow people to verbally abuse me or demean me

No swearing, cursing, or demeaning me

4. I will not allow people to vocationally abuse me or deny my right to worship

No excessive work or denial of worship

5. I will not allow people to use their authority or bitterness at authority to abuse me

No absolute submission and no unwarranted rebellion

6. I will not allow myself to be emotionally or physically abused

No leadership out of anger, violence, or threats of violence

7. I will not allow myself to be sexually abused

No sexual harm, exploitation, or infidelity

8. I will not allow myself to be financially abused or manipulated

No stealing, tricking, or defrauding,

9. I will not put up with people deceiving me for their own ends

No lying, deceiving, dishonesty

10. I will not allow people to mentally abuse me

No scheming against me – seeking to rob me of my personhood, possessions, or liberty

What are some dangers of being overly submissive (passive)?

Priorities out of order

Physical damage

Emotional damage

Mental damage

Spiritual damage

Unbalanced time allocation

Loss of personhood, value, and dignity

Unbalanced love

Unsuccessful lifestyle (Psalm 127)

Stress

Participation in evil

Approvers of evil

Channels for evil

Financial disaster

Missing God's will

Inability to say yes to God because you have not drawn adequate boundaries

Can you list other dangers?

Prayer of Righteous Submission

Heavenly Father,

I bow before you in the name of the Lord Jesus Christ and worship you for your wisdom in putting me under authority. First I thank you for your direct authority in my life and choose today to submit to your direction in my life. I will do what you prompt or direct me to do. I also thank you for the other authorities you have given me. I choose to do what they ask or desire as long as it does not violate your clearly revealed will. I realize that I have pushed hard against your direction through these authorities and that is wrong. I ask that the blood of Jesus Christ my Savior be used to cleanse me of that sin. I will live under my authorities' direction in their spheres of influence. I recognize that you have given me a mind which you want to use creatively under these people's authority. I also realize that you can even direct me through their mistakes. I ask that you, Heavenly Father, would specially work through my authorities to allow me to fully glorify you by causing me to reach my full potential. I thank you for seeking to develop in me the qualities of Christ in ways that I would never have chosen myself. I choose to cooperate with you. Thank You.

In the Name of the Lord Jesus Christ,

Amen

Turning Bitterness

into a

Forgiving Heart

Matthew 6:12-15; 18:21-35

Turning Bitterness into a Forgiving Heart ~ Matthew 6:12,14-15; 18:21-35

The goal of forgiveness is to be free from the damaging impact of the past. We may always carry the scars of the past, but we do not have to be imprisoned by them. Many people underestimate the need for forgiveness. Without forgiveness we are not pursuing our mission in life; we are trying to pay back the injustice of others. Many allow bitterness to become their reason for living rather than letting go of the offenses of others and finding their true purpose and their unique positive contribution. The joy of forgiveness is the ability to move on with our lives and not let the evil of others keep haunting us. God never designed us to carry bitterness. There is healing in forgiveness. There is justice in forgiveness. As long as we keep trying to hold a person responsible for the wrong they did to us, God and His proper authorities will not be free to work. Forgiveness is a conscious choice. Forgiveness begins with the desire to be free of the weight of justice personally. The exercises and projects that are listed in this section are designed to have you process what took place to you from various different angles and perspectives. Forgiveness involves three basic areas: 1) developing a forgiving heart that is able to let the offense go; 2) making sure that your conscience is clear in regard to this offense; 3) embracing the lessons and training that can come from this offense.

While the exercises below may seem impossible, they cause you to apply the principles of forgiveness found in the New Testament. This process will take time and will move you to think in new ways. However, being free from the enslaving attitudes of bitterness is worth it. Think of this time as being in a cocoon while you become a completely transformed person, able to forgive people and not letting their selfishness derail your future.

Write out a list of those who have deeply wounded you, what they did, and how often.

Most people do not have more than twenty people who have deeply wronged them; but if you do, then keep writing and noting what they did. We may have hundreds of people who have been rude, offensive, irritating and/or bothersome; but we usually have few who really have wounded us or wronged us deeply. They may have hurt us in a number of different ways at a number of different times. I have left two pages for these individuals and their offenses. I would suggest that you write using initials or in some code that only you will know so that these painful memories stay private until you are ready to reveal them.

Person   **Offense**

1.

2.

3.

4.

5.

6.

7.

8.

9.

10.

Determine whether what they did was wrong or just offensive.

In the process of letting go of bitterness it is important to label the nature of the offense. All societies have different levels of improper activities. These range from the criminal to the social. Let's spend some time looking at the types of offenses so we can label them more accurately. These are general categories and the definitions are decidedly broad. A **criminal offense** is where a person is harming others in some way and will most likely continue to harm others if they are not stopped. This would be like murder, rape, stealing, armed robbery, extortion. A **civil offense** is where the person has harmed another person in some way, but they may not continue doing it to others. This might be where one neighbor damaged their neighbor's fence, car, or dog for some reason. An **organizational offense** is where a person has offended, harmed, or hurt another person but their actions were a part of an organizational policy, order, or decision. This might be where a person is fired or reprimanded or reassigned by their employer. **Unethical offenses** are those offenses that are not technically or legally wrong but they are clearly selfish and wound or put the offended in a bad position. This might be where a person lies about their age on a form to get a leg up for a promotion or where a person uses their friendship with another person to push them ahead of a more qualified applicant for a promotion. An **accidental offense** is one in which the offender did not mean to do the action or did not understand that the action would result in what took place. This might be where a person did not know the brakes on the car were bad or they did not intend to lose control of the car as they sped out of the parking lot or they did not understand the power of the rifle or that it was loaded. A **familial offense** is a wound, hurt, or offense that takes place in a family or in a family's culture. This might be where a pet name used in a family becomes offensive to someone as they grow up. It may also be that a family ritual becomes offensive. A **religious offense** is an offense where the particular rituals, restrictions, or understandings of a religion are violated or made to be violated. This may be where a person is made to listen to blasphemies about their faith practices. It may be where a person is made to participate or watch what is forbidden by their religion. A **personal offense** is an offense that is personally offensive or harmful but not organizationally, civilly, or criminally liable. This may be a name or action that is used. It could be almost any action that another person continues to do after you have asked them to stop. An **everyday offense** is an offense, hurt, or wound that regularly takes place but does not rise to ethical or legal standards of wrong. This might be a slight, a word, an action, or an attitude that demeans you or marginalizes you from your point of view. Sometimes we are wounded or offended by another's actions, but their actions were not wrong. They just irritated you or were offensive in some other personal way. However, if their offenses were criminally wrong or morally wrong, then you are to declare them as wrong. Many people can never forgive or forget because they cannot label an offense as wrong. It might be because it is a loved one who committed it or because they feel responsible for the person. We must be willing to label an offense correctly. That was morally wrong!!! That was offensive!!! That was just irritating!!! That was criminal!!! Take each offense from the previous list and put it in a category below. Use the categories listed below to place the offense on a rough scale of evil. Let's take a look at the offenses in your life in more detail.

Who offended, wounded or hurt you?	Which kind of offense was it? criminal, civil, organizational, unethical, accidental, familial, religious, personal, every day	What action needs to be taken to stop, process, or fix this offense? If you don't know put DK

Who offended, wounded or hurt you?	Which kind of offense was it? criminal, civil, organizational, unethical, accidental, familial, religious, personal, every day	What action needs to be taken to stop, process, or fix this offense? If you don't know put DK

Tell God about your knowledge of their selfish motive. (Luke 19:21)

All sin comes from a core point of selfishness within a person. So those who have sinned against you were in some way just acting selfishly. Most people who sin are not trying to damage others; they are just trying to get what they want without regard for the consequences it will cause. It is important to realize that people have, at the core of their being, this principle of selfishness. It was supposed to be merely a self-interest and self-preservation instinct that was sublimated to God's glory and others good. But the fall of mankind stripped away our spiritual connection to God and made us lone wolves insensitive to others with our self-interest and self-preservation instincts dominant It is only by inviting God back into your life and using His energy to direct and repair your relationships that we can achieve health in this world. Remember, other people will wound you because of some personal desire, not because they want to destroy you. Make sure you are clear about the motivation of the offense: forgetfulness, selfishness, accidental, pent-up anger, addiction, etc. There is usually one prime selfish motivation for an offense.

It is very common to hear people who have caused awful things to happen to say with all sincerity, "That is not what I intended to happen." or "That is not what I wanted to happen." The person was just focused on what they wanted and did not stop to think of all the downstream consequences of this one action.

Jesus acknowledges this orientation towards the sins of others when He says while hanging on the cross. "Father, forgive them for they know not what they do." The people who were at that time crucifying him were just doing their jobs. They were being selfish even though they were killing the Son of God. He saw through their motives and asked the Father to pardon them because they did not understand the consequences of what they were doing.

I have asked many people to look at the offenses that have been done to them and to find the selfishness that always resides at the core of the offender's behavior. Why did this person do this thing? In most cases the person was not trying to damage others; they were just looking for what they wanted. It is true that at times a person does intentionally try to harm us but even that grows out of a selfish motive. Look at the list of the people and their offenses and identify the selfish thing the person was trying to do and say over them, "Father forgive them for they know not what they do."

YES, GOD I KNOW THAT THEY WERE JUST BEING SELFISH!!!

IN MANY CASES THEY DID NOT EVEN MEAN TO HURT ME – THEY WERE JUST BEING SELFISH

Maturing from the Offenses of Others

Romans 8:28,29 says that God causes all things to work together for good for those who love God, to those who are called according to His purpose. It is very helpful to start listing the good things that have come from the offense, the good things that could come from the offense, or the good things that might have come from this offense. Look for the ways that God is trying to bless you. This is not saying that the offense was good, it was not; but God is powerful enough to bless you in spite of this horrible thing. When we look for the ways that God wants to turn this bad thing into something good, we will begin seeing it.

Tell God that you want to know other ways this has been an open door for a blessing. For each offense list at least ten positive benefits.

Offense	Offense	Offense
1.	1.	1.
2.	2.	2.
3.	3.	3.
4.	4.	4.
5.	5.	5.
6.	6.	6.
7.	7.	7.
8.	8	8.
9.	9.	9.
10.	10.	10.
11.	11.	11.
12.	12.	12.
13.	13.	13.
14.	14.	14.
15.	15.	15.

Repeat this exercise for the other offenses that have been done to you. It is often in the looking for the good that we finally begin to see what has been there all along.

Give Vengeance to God Completely: Romans 12:17; Romans 13:4

A. Tell God what you would like to have happen to your offender.

Jesus tells us that we need to process the pain, loss, wounds, offenses, and sins of this life in Matthew 5:5 when He says "Blessed are those who mourn for they shall be comforted." Part of this processing of the pain may be telling God how devastated we were by the offense or how damaging the downstream consequences were of the offense. Another part of the mourning process is to tell God our feelings about the kind of punishments and justice we think should be done to the perpetrator. This is a therapeutic session between you and God where you are honest about the pain, the wound, and the changed life this person has caused. You bare your soul to God about the vengeance you think the person deserves. You are not scheming but suggesting. You know that ultimately God is the only one who can bring proper justice, but it is important that you bring your rage, bitterness, and thoughts out of yourself to the one being in the Universe who can handle them. This was done by David in Psalms in what are called the Imprecatory Psalms. He rails against his enemies and against the enemies of God. God can handle your raw emotions.

1.

2.

3.

4.

5.

6.

7.

8.

9.

10.

B. Tell God that you will leave Him any and all vengeance and/or justice

Many people want to forgive what the other person did, but they also want to pay back the person who did it to them. God tells us that we were not designed to handle bitterness and vengeance. (Romans 12:17-21; 13:4) It will eat us up inside and become a consuming reason to live. It is only in letting go of the delivery of justice that we will be truly free to live our lives and reach our potential. There is a real need to tell God in prayer that we are turning over to Him and His authorized agents all vengeance and justice for the perpetrator. Therefore, tell God that He has total control over what happens to them in terms of punishment.

Dear Lord Jesus,

I give you full permission to handle any punishment or correction that may need to be done to _____. I thank you that you are an all-seeing God who is too holy to overlook sin and too loving to be needlessly cruel. I release _____ into your hands and release my mind, will, emotions, words, and actions from seeking my own paybacks against _____. I will, Lord Jesus, for the security and safety of society, participate in civil justice if this is needed to send a message or for justice to be served in a moral wrong.

In the name of the Lord Jesus Christ,

Amen

Do this for each major offender in your life. The conversation with God around this prayer is important and liberating. The process of releasing the offender to God for His vengeance is not always easy. We must have an unshakable confidence in God's justice and in the fact that God knows all and saw the offense. It is possible that you may have this conversation with God a number of times because we all have a tendency to put ourselves back on vengeance patrol. But let God pursue the appropriate justice for the individual and get on with a great life that does not involve your offender or the memory of what they did.

1.	8.
2.	9.
3.	10.
4.	11.
5.	12.
6.	13.
7.	14.

Educate your offender about the consequences of their actions. Luke 19:21

The Scripture is clear that when someone sins against you, you have the right to educate them about the ways that they have sinned and the consequences of their selfishness. In the Bible this is called rebuking someone. We have come to see rebuke as scolding, yelling, or demeaning another person. But the main idea should be education. There needs to be an assumption that the person is not aware of all the ways that their actions, words, or attitudes have damaged others. Someone has to educate them. Yes, sometimes shame and guilt are a part of the education process. I have seen many people make great strides when they educate their offender about what happened after the sin. It is important that this be done in a safe environment and when the offended party is emotionally and spiritually ready to do it. Many sinful and selfish people have never had anyone actually help them see their actions, words, and attitudes from the other person's perspective. It can be a significant growth step for a wounded person to confront their offender with what they did and what happened. This does not have to be done, but there are many cases where this step of rebuking and educating your offender is important to letting it go.

Who do you need to rebuke or educate?

1.

2.

3.

4.

5.

Make a list of the unintended consequences that have come from this offense so that you will be able to be accurate when you educate your offender. You may have a conversation that goes something like, "I wanted to have you know that I remember what you did to me. You were just being selfish, but your actions really damaged my life. When you did that to me it caused these things to come into my life...

1.

2.

3.

4.

5.

"All of these things are on you because of what you did. I am trusting God for the energy to move forward and beyond your sinfulness to me."

Release your offenders so you can experience the forgiveness of God: Matthew 6:14,15

There is a clear statement in the prayer that Jesus taught his disciples that talks about forgiveness. "Forgive us our trespasses as we forgive those who trespass against us." There is some connection between our willingness to let go of the offenses of others and our experience of the forgiveness of God. Therefore it is important that we make the conscious choice to release others to God for any vengeance and justice. We must let God and His agents pursue the justice that our offenders are due. Open your soul to the forgiveness of God by forgiving others. Go through those who have offended you and release them to God and invite His forgiveness into your heart.

Dear Jesus,

I release my offender to you for all punishment and justice. I will help your agents gain justice when it is needed, but I want your forgiveness of my sins to surround me and uphold me. I need your touch of grace in my life, so I leave to you the offenses of others.

In the Name of the Lord Jesus Christ,

Amen

Suffering to meet needs: 1 Peter 2:19-25

In some instances, the selfishness of another exposes their desperate need for something. At times God calls us to meet those needs exposed by the suffering in order to turn off the selfishness in the person's life. Jesus suffered from our selfishness and condemnation "who for the joy set before Him endured the cross despised the shame and has sat down at the right hand of the throne of God" to meet our biggest need, which was the way back to God. The Apostle Peter tells us that at times Christians will be called upon to suffer so that right can be done, suffer so that one's selfishness can be stopped, suffer so that many can be saved. We have seen this kind of suffering for the greater good throughout the history of the church. Freemen selling themselves into slavery in order to share the good news of Christ's forgiveness with those isolated away in slavery; Christians volunteering to be thrown to the lions to protect the Bible; men and women turning their backs on promising careers to serve the poor, the afflicted and the oppressed; wives staying in marriages, that produce deep wounds, for the good of the children. God does not call everyone to this kind and level of suffering, but to some He does give this privilege. For most He calls us to a life of self-denial to show the grace and glory of Christ. Search the offense to see how many needs their offense represents which you could help heal

Ask God if there are any parts of the suffering you went through, are going through, or may go through that can allow some greater righteous need or good to be accomplished. Ask Him for the grace to endure and the wisdom to remain righteous in the suffering. Let God know you are willing to be His instrument to bring healing and righteousness. As you think through your offenders, make a list of the needs that their offense highlights. Think through how you could righteously meet the need that is causing them to be sinfully selfish.

1.

2.

3.

4.

5.

6.

7.

8.

9.

10.

Going the second mile: Matthew 5:38-42

Jesus tells us in the Sermon on the Mount that one of the ways to overcome bitterness is to invest more than is required in the person who is offending you. This is where Jesus says that if someone forces you to go one mile, go with him two miles. If someone sues you and wants to take your coat, give him your cloak also. We often try and give the least possible to those who have offended us and this in some cases keeps us bitter at our offender. Jesus tells us to become generous in our spirit towards the person and invest in them. I have found that if God wants you to make a second-mile investment in your offenders, He will let you know what your second mile project is. It could be helping them in their business. It could be buying something from them. It could be paying more in alimony than is required. It could be talking nicely and politely. It could be recommending them for a job. It could be giving them some money. There are literally hundreds of different second-mile investments that God might suggest we make. Each of them is designed to break our bitterness and produce a generous spirit toward our offender.

Tell God that you will invest in a second-mile project to overcome their or your resentment.

Commit yourself to God beforehand so that if He prompts you with a second-mile project you are already committed to doing it. One of the key ideas is that a second-mile investment is something beyond the common expected amount and displays a generous spirit and real love. Remember that second-mile projects never involve immorality or doing evil or violating any of God's clearly revealed will. Others might not completely agree with what God is telling you about a second-mile assignment, but it may be a crucial way to remove bitterness over a particular offender or offense. Make a list of potential second-mile projects for each offender.

Offender	Offender	Offender
1.	1.	1.
2.	2.	2.
3.	3.	3.
4.	4.	4.
5.	5.	5.
6.	6.	6.
7.	7.	7.
8.	8	8.
9.	9.	9.
10.	10.	10.

Pray all the positive you can for this person. Matthew 6:23-24.

When someone offends us we often can only focus on their mistakes and wrongs. We become so focused on the negative in their life that we cannot see the good or their needs. Unless we can change this single-minded focus on the bad, we will be unable to be free of their offense. One of the ways to do this is to pray positive into the lives of those who offend us. Jesus says to pray for those who persecute you, bless those who curse you, and love your enemies.

We want to break the negative emotional link between you and your offender by seeking to bless, pray, and love your enemy. See if you can help him/her succeed in a tangible way. One godly young woman I know found herself so troubled and bitter about some people at church that she began actually living out the verse "pray for those who persecute you." She went up to each of her persecutors and asked if there were things she could pray about for them. She diligently prayed for these people and after a few months her heart had changed towards them. What are the positive things that you could pray for your offenders?

Offender	Offender	Offender
1.	1.	1.
2.	2.	2.
3.	3.	3.
4.	4.	4.
5.	5.	5.
6.	6.	6.
7.	7.	7.
8.	8	8.
9.	9.	9.
10.	10.	10.

Heavenly Father,

*I right now today acknowledge my unforgiving heart. Lord Jesus, and I bow before you to release all my grudges, bitterness, and vengeance. I agree with you that I cannot become godly through bitterness. I have been held back in my Christian life. I seek to move forward, Lord Jesus, in intimacy with you and in service. Develop in me a forgiving spirit that is able to follow you regardless. I am asking you, blessed Holy Spirit, to cover me with your spirit for forgiveness and insight that I might be completely directed by you and walk as the blessed Lord Jesus Christ did, focused on the Father, ignoring the slights, offenses, and insults of those around Him. **Lord Jesus, come and live your life again in me today that I might be free.***

In the Name of the Lord Jesus Christ,

Amen

A Prayer of Confession

This is a suggested prayer of confession. Take each person and/or situation where you have developed bitterness, vengeance, or an unforgiving heart and admit to God that you were wrong. This is not a magical formula; it is a suggested prayer. But the ideas of confession, repentance, renunciation, cleansing, and transfer are powerful.. It is your sincerity and honesty before God that is important.

1. Confession and Repentance (1 John 1:9: 2 Timothy 2:24)

Lord Jesus, I agree with You that _____ is wrong. I turn away from it and ask that all the forgiveness that is in your death on Calvary be applied to my sin in this area. You say in your Word that _____ is wrong for you say _____. I realize that only in your power and through your direction can I successfully turn away from this sin.

2. Renunciation (2 Corinthians 4:4)

I repudiate, reject, and renounce any ground, place, or power I gave to Satan in my life through my involvement in _____. I give to the Lord Jesus Christ all power over this area of my life. I willingly surrender this area to the Lord Jesus Christ and the Holy Spirit.

3. Cleansing and Expulsion (1 John 1:9; Ephesians 4:27)

I cancel any contract I may have made with Satan through _____. I ask you, Lord Jesus, to cleanse me of any and all unrighteousness (including demons and demonic strongholds) because you say in your Word in 1 John 1:9 that "if we confess our sins He is faithful and just to forgive us our sins and to cleanse us of all unrighteousness."

4. Transfer of Ownership and Infusion of the Spirit of Truth (2 Corinthians 10:3-5; Colossians 1:27,28; Ephesians 5:18)

I right now transfer ownership of _____ in my life to the Lord Jesus Christ. I choose to take every thought regarding _____ captive to Christ (2 Corinthians 10:3-5) and allow Him full lordship in this area. I ask you, Lord Jesus, that you would fill this area of my life with the Holy Spirit of truth so that I would be wise, thankful, and able to see your plan in this area in the future. Thank you, Lord Jesus, for dying on the Cross for me. I choose to cooperate with you in _____ area of my life so that the process you began in me when I first trusted in You can continue. (Philippians 1:6). I realize that you want to display through me the character qualities of the Lord Jesus (Colossians 1:27,28; Galatians 2:20).

In the Name and for the Glory of the Lord Jesus Christ,

Amen

In order for a prayer of confession to be maximally effective in breaking very powerful satanic strongholds and influence, it is best if this prayer is prayed out loud with a mature Christian brother or sister who is watching you pray and is praying with and for you.

Developing a clear conscience. 1 Timothy 1:18-20; Luke 17:3

A clear conscience means that we have made every attempt to apologize, make right, and repair damage that we have done to others. The Scriptures tells us that as far as it depends on us, we have made peace with everyone whom we have wronged (Romans 12:18). We want to continue the process of developing a forgiving heart by developing a clear conscience which is essential for a servant of Christ (1 Timothy 1:18-20). Without a clear conscience, one cannot be sensitive to the Holy Spirit as He guides us through life. One of the key places that we sense the Holy Spirit is in our conscience. When our conscience is clean without offense before God or man that we know of, we are able to understand and respond to the Holy Spirit better.

How to clear your conscience. Luke 17:3

Write out a list of all those who you have wronged. Cleaning up the messes of the past is important soul work. Often we cannot let go of bitterness until we have apologized for our part in the episode. It is not whether you can repair all damage or restore every relationship; it is that you are acknowledging that you did wrong and you want to clean up the mess you made.

1.

2.

3.

4.

5.

6.

7.

8.

9.

10.

Write out a list of all those who were once close but are now distant.

Sometimes we cannot think of people we have offended or wrongs we have committed because we have blocked them out of our memory. One of the ways to look a little deeper into our past in order to clear up past offenses is to look at folks who were once close to us but are now distant or strained in their relationship with us. This can occur because of something we did. It can be helpful to indicate a potential reason for the distance.

Some people can go overboard on this assignment and write down any one who is not super close to them. For some of us, our perfectionism or self-loathing can condemn us in every direction because of an exercise like this. Do not let that happen. God loves you and died on the cross for you. You are trying to make sure that you have cleared up – as far as it depends on you – any major offenses between you and others. This exercise is designed to uncover major hurts, wounds, and damage that you have caused, not minor offenses. If you did not say Hello in the seventh grade to someone in the hallway, let it go. If you didn't like someone in high school and gave them dirty looks, let it go. Do not beat yourself up over small things. Look for the big offenses where your actions, words, or attitudes did significant damage. Let the small stuff go.

1.

2.

3.

4.

5.

6.

7.

8.

9.

10.

Prepare to contact the people you have wronged and the ones who are distant and seek to understand (education) in what ways you might have offended them.

Warning: In some cases it may be unsafe for you to contact some of the people you have wronged. If it will do damage to the other person or damage to you, then make sure that you work with your mentor and wise counsel before you make the contact.

People will help you understand how you offended them if they are convinced that you really want to change and not commit that type of offense again. If we are to be sincere disciples of Christ, then we must be committed to growth and movement toward Christlikeness.

Seek a Rebuke

When you first begin to talk with this person who you offended, they are wondering why you want to talk so let them know. "I am calling because I have come to realize that I really hurt you, and I would like to apologize for that and make it right if I can. I know I probably don't really understand all the ways that I have hurt or damaged you, so I am hopeful that you can help me understand so that I never hurt anyone else like that again." Then you pause and wait for their reply. This is called seeking a rebuke (Luke 17:3). In other words you must ask others to educate you on how you offended them. This means asking them to tell you and preparing yourself to not defend yourself if they do tell you. This is never an easy step and means that you must be willing to listen as they tell you what happened from their side of the story. They hate you or add things to the story that are not true. Listen all the way through without interrupting their telling of their version of what you did or did not to them with all the emotions that may come with the retelling. You asked for the rebuke and you need to hear and feel what they felt and heard. Only after you have heard it can you suggest that there may be some details that may need to be cleared up (if they were wrong). If the essential facts are true, do not quibble about a trivial detail. Do not try and tell a person that they should feel differently than they do. If there is a huge element that they have misunderstood or something that they believe is true that is not, then you can humbly suggest that there has been a misunderstanding. You can then ask if they would like you to clear it up. They may be so mad at you or distrusting of you that they do not want you to give them any information. You may just have to humbly apologize for the general offenses and not deal with specific details because the two of you disagree about them.

You must be gentle in spirit (Proverbs 15:1). You can never expect that people will really help you understand how you have offended them if your spirit, voice, and facial expression do not say that you are humble and ready to learn. They must really sense that you want to know. This means, on your part, you must see the relationship as more important than your pride, your way, and your ease. It will be difficult to hear your offense from their point of view, but it is essential if you are to learn and they are to release the offense and heal the distance.

They will toss out a few safe offenses to see if you are listening before they give you the real one. It is often true that people will see if you are listening by telling of some small offenses that may or may not relate to the real offense. If they see that you are really seeking to understand and change, they will share the larger offense with you.

Do not defend yourself or try and clarify any misunderstandings at this point. You must take a non-defensive posture in these times. It is best to approach them as though you were a recorder writing down a list of grievances about someone else other than yourself. If you do have an explanation for why a particular thing happened, save the explanation until after they are finished and they realize that you can to listen.

Make the contact… don't put it off… make the call… do not put it in a letter… They need to see or hear your sincerity. The one exception to this step of contacting those whom you have offended is do not do this if it is unsafe for you or unsafe for them.

Relive your offense through their eyes.

You must feel the offense from their point of view. Often having them tell you the offense from their point of view is enough for them to realize you are really apologetic. At other times you must spend time reflecting on how much your offense would have hurt if you had been in their place. It is only after you have really grappled with your offense from their eyes that they can forgive you. You can relate it to a similar experience in your life if that helps. They must know that you realize how offensive your actions were.

Do not let yourself reduce the importance of your offense by hiding behind what they did first. When you look at what you did, do not rationalize that you were forced to do it because... You are seeking to clear up what you did, not blame them for what they did. Realize that you had a choice and you did what you did. Take responsibility for what you did. You may have to list out the options that you could have done in response to their actions or the actions that preceded your doing what you did.

1.

2.

3.

4.

5.

6.

7.

8.

9.

10.

Agree with them concerning your offense (confession). Luke 17:3

Realize that they may see your offense as bigger they you do. Ask yourself how big they see your offense in terms of causing the distance between you and them. ____%. The offense that they are holding against you may seem much smaller to you, but it is not to them.

Tell them you were wrong for what you did. State clearly without any excuses that you realize that you were wrong for what you did. Do not imply or say that they were wrong also. Do not say, "If I was wrong, please forgive me." Admit you were wrong.

Clarify what took place if a genuine misunderstanding has taken place, but only in a spirit of humility and gentleness. Always give them the benefit of the doubt. If you believe that there was a misunderstanding or they are just not aware of something that would change their minds, it is most helpful to share it in the fashion: "I may be mistaken, but I think that there are a few things you may not be aware of that will explain why I did what I did. May I explain?"

Remember the goal here is to clear up what you did that was wrong not to hash out exactly who did what to whom and how much blame should be assigned to what action. Confession is agreeing with the other person regarding your actions, words, or attitude in a situation. Remember the goal is to clear up your offenses. They will have to deal with their issues on their own.

If the offense is serious, or has occurred regularly and involves a continuing relationship, you may need to agree to repentance plan (repentance). Luke 3:8; 17:3

One of the most difficult problems in this area of forgiveness is the problem of repeated offenses. If you admit that you were wrong and do not want to commit the offense again but you repeatedly offend someone, your apology will not seem valid. This is when a repentance plan comes in to play. We often need some penalty or consequences that can be administered to remind us to stop doing the offense. We may come up with a way that the penalty will be administered if we re-offend. Just like with training children, the penalty must be significant enough to cause a person to change their behavior. What are possible repentance plans for our repeated offenses?

Let me suggest a few small ones. One man who consistently made a mess in the kitchen and did not clean it up agreed with his wife that if he did it again he would do all the Sunday dishes. One woman who overspent the family budget was forced to surrender her credit card for a month if it happened again. One man who looked at pornography on the computer put watching software on the computer and was not allowed on the computer after 10 p.m.

1.

2.

3.

4.

5.

This may mean or involve restitution. Repentance also involves restitution if the offense involved the destruction, stealing, or incapacitation of real property or money. Your repentance plan may include paying back twice* what the item was worth.

Ask them to forgive you. Luke 17:3

Pose the question, "Will you forgive me?" Wait for a response. You need to hear them say yes. There is something powerful about hearing another person verbally say that they forgive you. This act of verbal forgiveness helps them and it helps you. They may need time to see if you are genuinely serious about your desire to stop offending them. Let them have the time. Forgiveness is not something you can demand because you followed a few prearranged steps. It is rather a privilege granted by the offended party.

If they chose not to forgive you, then you may have to start again on the education step with an even gentler spirit or work on the repentance plan. Sometimes you need to let them have a part in developing the repentance plan. Often they do not think you mean it, that you will not really change, or that you do not really understand how much it hurt. They may need time before their heart can let go of the pain you caused. The main thing is that you have done what you could to make amends. Do not let their lack of forgiveness hold you back. Move forward on a life of increasing love and grace.

It is possible that they will not forgive you because of their own hard hearts, or what it would mean they would have to do, or because then they would have to ask forgiveness of you. If that is the case, then you have sought to be at peace with all men as far as it depends on you.

It is important that you have sought forgiveness from those you have offended. As you have done this, your soul becomes less burdened. Embrace the wonder of forgiveness that Christ offers and pour that forgiveness to others.

As you look at doing this step, pray the prayer of confession to God that is on the next page. This can act like a warm-up to speaking with the person you offended. This whole process will be a huge blow to your pride, but it will be a crucial step for your soul. Pray to the Lord, but start the process of being clean between you and others.

Do not put off doing this step. It will be a very difficult step to talk to the people whom you have deeply offended and hurt. You have been prepped with what to say and what to do by the material you have just read. Take the first person on the list and make the phone call. The whole phone call may not last long, but it will be the beginning of a wonderful process of being free from what you did.

A Prayer of Confession

This is a suggested prayer of confession. Take each person and/or situation where you have developed bitterness, vengeance or an unforgiving heart and admit to God that you were wrong. This is not a magical formula; it is a suggested prayer. But the ideas of confession, repentance, renunciation, cleansing, and transfer are powerful. It is your sincerity and honesty before God that is important.

1. Confession and Repentance (1 John 1:9: 2 Timothy 2:24)

Lord Jesus, I agree with You that _____ is wrong. I turn away from it and ask that all the forgiveness that is in your death on Calvary be applied to my sin in this area. You say in your Word that _____ is wrong for you say _____. I realize that only in your power and through your direction can I successfully turn away from this sin.

2. Renunciation (2 Corinthians 4:4)

I repudiate, reject, and renounce any ground, place, or power I gave to Satan in my life through my involvement in _____. I give to the Lord Jesus Christ all power over this area of my life. I willingly surrender this area to the Lord Jesus Christ and the Holy Spirit.

3. Cleansing and Expulsion (1 John 1:9; Ephesians 4:27)

I cancel any contract I may have made with Satan through _____. I ask you, Lord Jesus, to cleanse me of any and all unrighteousness (including demons and demonic strongholds) because you say in your Word in 1 John 1:9 that "if we confess our sins He is faithful and just to forgive us our sins and to cleanse us of all unrighteousness."

4. Transfer of Ownership and Infusion of the Spirit of Truth (2 Corinthians 10:3-5; Colossians 1:27,28; Ephesians 5:18)

I right now transfer ownership of _____ in my life to the Lord Jesus Christ. I choose to take every thought regarding _____ captive to Christ (2 Corinthians 10:3-5) and allow Him full lordship in this area. I ask you, Lord Jesus, that you would fill this area of my life with the Holy Spirit of truth so that I would be wise, thankful, and able to see your plan in this area in the future. Thank you, Lord Jesus, for dying on the Cross for me. I choose to cooperate with you in _____ area of my life so that the process you began in me when I first trusted in You can continue. (Philippians 1:6). I realize that you want to display through me the character qualities of the Lord Jesus (Colossians 1:27,28; Galatians 2:20).

In the Name and for the Glory of the Lord Jesus Christ,

Amen

In order for a prayer of confession to be maximally effective in breaking very powerful satanic strongholds and influence, it is best if this prayer is prayed out loud with a mature Christian brother or sister who is watching you pray and is praying with and for you.

Here is a general prayer about developing a forgiving heart.

Heavenly Father,

I right now, today, acknowledge my unforgiving heart, Lord Jesus, and I bow before you to release all my grudges, bitterness, and vengeance. I agree with you that I cannot become godly through bitterness. I have been held back in my Christian life. I seek to move forward, Lord Jesus, in intimacy with you and in service. Develop in me a forgiving spirit that is able to follow you regardless. I am asking you, blessed Holy Spirit, to cover me with your spirit for forgiveness and insight that I might be completely directed by you and walk as the blessed Lord Jesus Christ did, focused on the Father, ignoring the slights, offenses, and insults of those around Him.

Lord Jesus, come and live your life in me today that I might be free.
In the name of the Lord Jesus Christ,
Amen

Turning Lust

into a Pure Heart

Matthew 5:38; 2 Timothy 2:22, 1 Corinthians 6:18,19

Overcoming Lust and Developing a Pure Heart Matthew 5:38; 2 Timothy 2:22, 1 Corinthians 6:18,19

Purity is about thinking, speaking, and acting in a pure manner. There is an amazing joy and liberation in purity. Purity is being truly beneficial to yourself, others, and society. Purity is not always what we want but it is what we need. Deep inside we crave purity and the life-giving energy it gives. There is great joy and peace in being pure. Think about eating pure life-giving healthy food. Think about breathing pure life-giving healthy air. Think about drinking pure life-giving healthy water. Purity gives life. Purity brings health. Purity reenergizes and restores. Too often in Christian circles we think of purity in terms of what it is not. This approach can cause us to fixate on what we don't want to do, say, or think. But sometimes that causes us to focus on the impure. Purity is about the joy, health, and peace of positive personal and relational behavior. There are hundreds of things that are damaging, destructive, and poisonous that need to be eliminated; but we must be focused on purity. To pursue purity is to go after the actions, thoughts, or words that will be the most beneficial to ourselves and to the others. Becoming pure is not about saying no as much as it is about saying yes to healthy relationships, yes to life-giving thoughts, yes to deep intimacy with God, yes to soul-enriching activities, yes to restorative community activities. It is almost impossible to win against impurity by focusing on saying NO. But it is possible to grow more and more in purity by aiming at healthy relationships, healthy thought patterns, healthy activities, and life-giving good works. In order to be pure you will have to say no to what is toxic, draining, and poisonous to your life and relationships, but the focus is not on NO.

With this understanding it is possible to grasp what lust is. Lust is inordinate desire for anything, anyone, or any activity that destroys health, purity, peace, and joy in your life. Lust is inordinate desire for what is impure — for what will damage ourselves, others, or society. There are hundreds of actions, thoughts, and words that seem exciting and pleasurable, but they do significant damage to us or to others or to the society at large. This is what lust is.

Let me give you an example: There are things (pornography, affairs, strip clubs, prostitutes) that a man can pursue that will significantly damage his wife and/or his children. They may be very enjoyable things for him but very damaging for the family. He may not be significantly damaged by doing them. He may enjoy the activity so much that He does not mind any damage that accrues to him personally. If he focuses on how much he enjoys doing these things, then he will always be tempted to do them even though his family will suffer. The question becomes: How can I have a pure, healthy, life-giving marriage and family? The pursuit of a great marriage is the goal. He will have to give up some things in order to have the wonder of a great marriage.

Lust is pursuing something toxic to ourselves or others. It doesn't matter how much we like it or whether we can handle it. The question is what that pursuit does to you, to the relationships of your life, to the society at large.

Let me give you a few other examples: Someone may really like shopping and spending money. It helps their mood, keeps them happy. But no matter how much they enjoy it, if their family does not have the money to pay for what they buy then their fun thing will destroy the family's security and stability. If someone enjoys listening and spreading the problems of others, it does not matter how much they enjoys this activity, they may be damaging their relationships and others' ability to trust them. If someone enjoys a hobby so much that they spend lots of time and/or money so that family needs are left undone, then the hobby has become a toxic thing.

Usually when a person is pursuing some impure thing that is damaging, there is some enjoyable, pure activity that they are completely missing. At times people feel that if they give up the destructive impure thing, there is nothing to do but be bored. This is never the case. Purity is more exciting and life-giving than impurity. We just have to find the activities, thoughts, and words of purity. We all want to receive pure, encouraging, positive words, thoughts, and actions from others because these are so life-giving. There is purity all around us. We have just been trained to notice impurity. Impurity is screaming at us so that we will not see the purity that is so much better for us. Make no mistake, there are toxic elements in our society that will destroy the individual, marriages, families, and even the communities of the people who pursue them. The usual impure suspects are alcohol, drugs, prostitution, gambling, pornography, and the like.

Jesus does not want us to be focused on saying no to lust but instead to say yes to purity. Matthew 5:6; 8 It is purity that heals. It is purity that brings joy. It is purity that brings stability and health. What does a pure romantic relationship look like? What does a pure positive parent-child relationship look like? What does a pure positive energetic worker look like? When you can answer what purity looks like, then you can pursue it. It is not enough to try and stay away from impurity. My wife wants me to do so much more in our marriage than stay away from affairs and pornography. She and I both want a live-giving, pure relationship of love that fills our soul and energizes our lives. Of course that kind of relationship avoids affairs and pornography.

Describe a healthy, positive, pure life-giving relationship

If you are going to utilize the grace of God to build and enjoy a pure life, then you must know what that life looks like. Olympic athletes decide that they want to be Olympians and what it will look and feel like to experience that achievement. They think of the skills, times, scores, and accomplishments that they will need to achieve to become an Olympian. Then they eliminate the things that will not let them get to those places. In the same way, if you want the blessing of God, the peace of God, and the healthy relationships that God promises, you must go after these positive pure goals and eliminate what will keep you from getting there. It is not as hard to eliminate something you like doing if you know what you want to accomplish. Go for purity; it is worth it.

What does purity look like in your relationship with God?

What does impurity look like in your relationship with God?

What does a pure relationship with yourself look like?

What does an impure relationship with yourself look like?

What does a pure marriage relationship look like?

What does an impure marriage relationship look like?

What does a pure family relationship look like?

What does an impure family relationship look like?

What does a pure work life look like?

What does an impure work look like?

What does a pure relationship with your friends look like?

What does an impure relationship with your friends look like?

Describe what a positive, pure relationship looks like in each of these major areas of life

It can be very helpful to think about a pure life as a life full of righteous love. This is what Jesus says that He wants our lives to be like. Think and pray about the following questions and how God guides you in them.

What does it really mean to love God with all your heart, soul, mind, and strength?

What does it mean to love yourself with a righteous love spiritually, mentally, emotionally, physically?

What does it mean to love your spouse (or future spouse if you are not married) and developing a deep enjoyable love life together?

What does it mean to love your family (immediate and extended)?

What does it mean to love your friends (close, casual, acquaintance, and frenemies)?

What does it mean to love your work mates (boss, colleagues, subordinates)?

What does it mean to respect your money and not let it become love?

Growing in purity

It is important to know what purity looks and feels like. We often learn far more about what we really want in life from watching people who are doing it well. Without mentors and role models, it is much harder to grasp life-giving purity. Who are mentors or role models of a life-giving mentor in each of the key relationships? If you have more than one, that is great. Put them all down and write down what makes them a role model.

	Mentors/Role Models	Potential Mentors / Role models
God		
Self-Development		
Marriage/Romance		
Family		
Work		
Church		
Finances		
Friends		

If you don't have any role models in an area, then that may be an area of great struggle because you have no one to show you how it is done. Don't be afraid to ask people to be your mentors or role models.

Making life-giving movies in your head. Philippians 4:8

The Scriptures are clear that we are to reject evil, impure, and damaging thoughts and images; but we can only reject them if we have something more powerful and compelling to think about instead. Notice that the Scriptures says in Philippians 4:8 *whatever is true, whatever is honorable, whatever is right, whatever is pure, whatever is lovely, whatever is of good repute, if there is any excellence and if anything worthy of praise, think on these things.* When temptation comes at us, we need to be prepared with mental images of great times with our spouse, deeply joyful times with our children, exciting righteous times having fun, encouraging times of success and achievement, or overwhelming times with the Lord. If we have not had these memories, then make movies of these times about the future. When it is time to say no to temptation, we must say yes to great movies of righteous, pure things.

Realize the Battle is for your mind. Matthew 5:28, 2 Corinthians 10:3-5

The battle is for your mind. The images, fantasies, thoughts, and ideas that you allow your mind to think about are what will control your behavior. We will do what we think about most of the time. We are responsible for the thoughts we allow our mind to think. Many have not considered this. The mind is not a morality-free zone where anything that goes on in your mind cannot be considered wrong because it is only in your mind. But you do not have to let every stray thought that comes through your mind stay there and grow. What you think about is what you will become. If you think about being greedy all the time, you will become greedy. If you think about being a loving, gracious, and kind person all the time, then you will become a loving, gracious, and kind person. The battle for what kind of life you will enjoy or be cursed with is in the mind. What do you let your mind think about and what kind of person do you see yourself? Proverbs 23:7 "For as a man thinks in his heart so is he." Proverbs 14:14 "The backslider in heart will have his fill of his own ways."

Many people are discouraged because they are not able to conquer the habits that we know are wrong. They are unaware that they are fighting the wrong battle. Impure actions are a by-product of impure thoughts. Only as the battle is won in the thought life will there be hope of victory in actions.

When you are tempted you must have positive, pure, delightful images, and ideas that you can think about instead of tempting ones. What are your most positive powerful righteous memories in each of these areas?

In each area remember or plan a few delightful memories that you can force your mind to dwell on so that you will not be thinking about the temptation.

God	Work
Self-Development	Church
Marriage/Romance	Finances
Family	Friends

We all do this. It is called day dreaming about something that is really cool. It could be about something we did before or something we want to do. The key here is to make sure it is delightful and pure. It has to capture your attention more than the temptation.

Moving from lust to purity

In this next section we will be suggesting exercises to move away from lust and toward purity. You may do all of these exercises or just a few selected ones. Further exercises in this area are in the book, *Mission Possible: Winning the Battle Over Temptation.* Purity requires shaking free from all mental, physical, emotional, and spiritual entanglements which hinder you from doing the right thing (Hebrews 12:1-3).

What are activities, actions, words, and thoughts that could keep you from a positive, pure, life-giving relationship in the major areas of life? Go ahead and look at each area and write down what may be blocking the best in that relationship.

God	Self Development	Marriage/ Dating	Family	Work	Church	Finances	Friends

Confessing your sexual sins. 1 John 1:9; Matt 5:11

Listed below are the sexual sins that are destructive to a healthy marriage, family, and individual. Look at the list and pray a prayer of confession for the sins that you have been involved in. If you do not know about something on the list, do not worry about that one. You have most likely not sinned in that way.

Pornography: Leviticus 18:6-18

Mental Adultery: Matthew 5:28

Transvestitism (Cross Dressing): Deuteronomy 22:5

Physical Defrauding During Dating: Galatians 5:19

Masturbation: Galatians 5:19: Romans 1:20-31

Pre-Marital Episodes: Deuteronomy 22:22-29

Adultery: Leviticus 20:10-12: Deuteronomy 22:22

Prostitution: Deuteronomy 22:17-18

Immoral Conduct, Indecent Exposure, Voyeurism: Deuteronomy 22:17-18

Homosexual Episodes: Leviticus 18:22,20:13

Incest: Leviticus 18:6-18,20:14

Bestiality: Leviticus 18:23,20:15,16

Incubus and Succubus (Spiritistic Sexuality): Genesis 6:3, Jude 1:6

Necrophilia: Numbers 19:13

Sacrificial Sexuality: Leviticus 18:21, 20:6 Deuteronomy 19:14

Turn to the next page and pray the prayer of confession over each of the times you have sinned in these ways. There is something very powerful about admitting to God that you have been involved in significant sexual, selfish behavior. Remember that there is forgiveness in Jesus the Christ. He is not waiting to condemn but to comfort and forgive those who admit that they have been destroying their own lives by going beyond God's plan for sexuality.

A Prayer of Confession

This is a suggested prayer of confession. Take each person and/or situation where you have gone outside of God's plan for sexuality and admit to God that you were wrong. This is not a magical formula; it is a suggested prayer. But the ideas of confession, repentance, renunciation, cleansing, and transfer are powerful. It is your sincerity and honesty before God that is important.

1. Confession and Repentance (1 John 1:9: 2 Timothy 2:24)

Lord Jesus, I agree with You that _____ is wrong. I turn away from it and ask that all the forgiveness that is in your death on Calvary be applied to my sin in this area. You say in your Word that _____ is wrong for you say _____. I realize that only in your power and through your direction can I successfully turn away from this sin.

2. Renunciation (2 Corinthians 4:4)

I repudiate, reject, and renounce any ground, place, or power I gave to Satan in my life through my involvement in _____. I give to the Lord Jesus Christ all power over this area of my life. I willingly surrender this area to the Lord Jesus Christ and the Holy Spirit.

3. Cleansing and Expulsion (1 John 1:9; Ephesians 4:27)

I cancel any contract I may have made with Satan through _____. I ask you, Lord Jesus, to cleanse me of any and all unrighteousness (including demons and demonic strongholds) because you say in your Word in 1 John 1:9 that "if we confess our sins He is faithful and just to forgive us our sins and to cleanse us of all unrighteousness."

4. Transfer of Ownership and Infusion of the Spirit of Truth (2 Corinthians 10:3-5; Colossians 1:27,28; Ephesians 5:18)

I right now transfer ownership of _____ in my life to the Lord Jesus Christ. I choose to take every thought regarding _____ captive to Christ (2 Corinthians 10:3-5) and allow Him full lordship in this area. I ask you, Lord Jesus, that you would fill this area of my life with the Holy Spirit of truth, so that I would be wise, thankful, and able to see your plan in this area in the future. Thank you, Lord Jesus, for dying on the Cross for me. I choose to cooperate with you in _____ area of my life so that the process you began in me when I first trusted in You can continue. (Philippians 1:6). I realize that you want to display through me the character qualities of the Lord Jesus (Colossians 1:27,28; Galatians 2:20).

In the Name and for the Glory of the Lord Jesus Christ, Amen

In order for a prayer of confession to be maximally effective in breaking very powerful satanic strongholds and influence, it is best if this prayer is prayed out loud with a mature Christian brother or sister who is watching you pray and is praying with and for you.

GIVE GOD'S SPIRIT HIS MOST EFFECTIVE WEAPON: PSALMS 119:10-11

Temptation is like a toxic wind that blows into your life and seeks to corrupt the righteousness and love in your life. When you put Scripture in your mind, it is like a powerful wind that blows against these toxic winds and does not let these poisonous elements reach us. We are protected by the truth that is in our hearts. Psalm 119:10, 11 says it well when it says, "How shall a young man keep his way pure? By keeping it according to Thy word. Thy word I have hid in my heart that I might not sin against Thee."

There is something very powerful that begins to happen when we memorize and meditate on the Scriptures as opposed to just reading the word. God's Word, when it is inside of us, begins to work on us, in us, and through us as well as drawing the blessing of God. Psalms 1:3 says that if we meditate on the law of God, we will be like a tree firmly planted by streams of water, which yields its fruit in season and its leaf does not wither and whatever he does he prospers. This incredible promise of growth, strength, and development because we have taken in the Word of God is not just words but it is truth and life. God will work to bless us and make us shine out His glory because we have been meditating on Him.

Memorize the following verses by slowly reading them out loud ten times and then trying to say them from memory three times during the day – potentially at breakfast, lunch, and dinner. When you have memorized one, then move on the next one no matter how many days it takes to memorize the first one; just stay with it. Then when you have memorized it, move on. Put a check mark by the verse when you have memorized and recited this verse to someone.

- o 1 Corinthians 3:13 *Each man's work will become evident; for the day will show it because it is to be revealed with fire, and the fire itself will test the quality of each man's work.*

- o 2 Corinthians 10:3-5 *For though we walk in the flesh, we do not war according to the flesh, for the weapons of our warfare are not of the flesh, but divinely powerful for the destruction of fortresses. We are destroying speculations and every lofty thing raised up against the knowledge of God, and we are taking every thought captive to the obedience of Christ.*

- o James 1:2-4 *Consider it all joy, my brethren, when you encounter various trials, knowing that the testing of your faith produces endurance. And let endurance have its perfect result, so that you may be perfect and complete, lacking in nothing.*

- o 1 Thessalonians 4:3-5 *For this is the will of God, your sanctification; that is, that you abstain from sexual immorality; that each of you know how to possess his own vessel in sanctification and honor, not in lustful passion, like the Gentiles who do not know God.*

- o Romans 6:11-13 *Even so consider yourselves dead to sin but alive to God in Christ Jesus. Therefore do not let sin reign in your mortal body so that you obey its lusts, and do not go on presenting the members of your body to sin as instruments of unrighteousness; but present yourselves to God as those alive from the dead, and your members as instruments of righteousness to God.*

- o Galatians 5:16 *But I say, walk by the Spirit, and you will not carry out the desire of the flesh.*

133

o Galatians 5:22,23 *But the fruit of the Spirit is love, joy, peace, patience, kindness, goodness, faithfulness, gentleness, self-control; against such things there is no law.*

o Galatians 5:24 *Now those who belong to Christ Jesus have crucified the flesh with its passions and desires.*

o Colossians 3:2,5 *Set your mind on the things above, not on the things that are on earth. Therefore consider the members of your earthly body as dead to immorality, impurity, passion, evil desire, and greed, which amounts to idolatry.*

o Hebrews 12:11,12 *All discipline for the moment seems not to be joyful, but sorrowful; yet to those who have been trained by it, afterwards it yields the peaceful fruit of righteousness. Therefore, strengthen the hands that are weak and the knees that are feeble*

o Psalm 1:1-3 *How blessed is the man who does not walk in the counsel of the wicked, nor stand in the path of sinners, nor sit in the seat of scoffers! But his delight is in the law of the Lord, and in His law he meditates day and night. He will be like a tree firmly planted by streams of water, which yields its fruit in its season and its leaf does not wither; and in whatever he does, he prospers.*

o Proverbs 15:3 *The eyes of the Lord are in every place, watching both the evil and the good.*

o Psalm 119:9,11 *How can a young man keep his way pure? By keeping it according to Your word. Your word I have treasured in my heart, That I may not sin against You.*

o Judges 16:21 *Then the Philistines seized him and gouged out his eyes; and they brought him down to Gaza and bound him with bronze chains, and he was a grinder in the prison.*

o Psalm 19:14 *Let the words of my mouth and the meditation of my heart be acceptable in Your sight, O Lord, my rock and my Redeemer.*

o Job 31:1 *I have made a covenant with my eyes, how then could I gaze at a virgin?*

o Romans 12:1,2 *Therefore I urge you, brethren, by the mercies of God, to present your bodies a living and holy sacrifice, acceptable to God, which is your spiritual service of worship. And do not be conformed to this world, but be transformed by the renewing of your mind, so that you may prove what the will of God is, that which is good and acceptable and perfect.*

REMOVE HIDDEN PROVISIONS FOR DEFEAT. ROMANS 13:14

When Captain Cook sailed his ships into Hawaii, in order to explore the islands and because he did not want his men to be tempted to retreat back to the ships, he burnt the ships so there was no going back. Many times we leave in our life ways of giving into temptation because we really want to fall back into those ways again. I have watched alcoholics hide a bottle of vodka in the toilet tank. I have watched people who are committed to losing weight hide Oreo cookies in the linen closet so in case they are desperate, they will be able to find some food. I had a man who took all the pornography from his home when I told him to remove it. But he put it in his truck because it was worth so much and he didn't really want to part with it. There is a part of us that is very drawn to particular temptations and sins that we have committed in the past. We often allow ourselves vulnerable places where we could fall into temptation and sin because we really want to. If we are going to be honest with God and ourselves, we must eliminate all of these hidden provisions for sin. Only you know what and where they all are. If you are serious, you must remove these.

Images, Movies, Pornography

Relationships

Reminders

Equipment

Use the spiritual truth that, "You can't do two things at the same time." Galatians 5:16

It is absolutely true that if you are doing the right thing, then you can't be doing the wrong thing. It is also true that if you are doing the wrong thing, then you are not doing the right thing. This is the basis for this Scripture that tells us that if we are following the promptings of the Holy Spirit, we will not be giving into temptations that we know are wrong. The quicker you can start doing what the Lord is prompting, the faster you will be free from the power of the temptation. What will you do instead of what you have done?

1.

2.

3.

4.

Count on and look for God's way of escape 1 Corinthians 10:13

In what ways has the Lord provided ways of escape in the past?

1.

2.

3.

4.

5.

6.

7.

8.

9.

10.

GET A HANDLE ON THE INFLUENCES OF YOUR LIFE

If we are ever going to reach our maximal potential and succeed as God would have us, we must come to grips with the principle of influence. We are in large measure the product influences have been or are a part of our lives. We have control over many of those influences. If we choose wisely, then we will be propelled toward wisdom and righteousness. If we choose poorly or not at all, then we will be driven to wickedness and folly. If you want to get a firm grip on doing something with your life and becoming successful, then understand and work with the principle of influence. We must live in the real world, not the one we want to live in or the one that people have said is real. It is not true when you say, "Oh, that does not affect me." You may not be aware of how it affects you. You may not be as much affected by that as someone else. You may be affected in a positive way. However, you are still affected. We must open our eyes to see that all things exert an influence on our lives and should be examined in terms of what type of influence they exert. We must realize that every day of our lives is a battle for our minds because:

EVERYTHING INFLUENCES YOU!!!!

EVERY PERSON, CHOICE, MEMORY, SITUATION

INFLUENCES YOU EITHER TO GOOD OR EVIL

OR

TO WISDOM OR TO FOLLY.

We do not have a choice whether something will influence us; we only have a choice whether to allow that thing into our lives to exert its influence. The more we surround ourselves with positive influences, the more we will please God in all we think, say, and do.

Read what the Scripture says about influences:

Matthew 5:29,30 *If your right eye makes you stumble, tear it out, and throw it from you; for it is better for you that one of the parts of your body perish, than for your whole body to be thrown into hell. And if your right hand makes you stumble, cut if off and throw if from you; for it is better for you that one of the parts of your body perish, than for your whole body to go into hell.*

1 Corinthians 15:33 *Do not be deceived; bad company corrupts good morals.*

Philippians 4:8 *Finally, brethren, whatever is true, whatever is honorable, whatever is right, whatever is pure, whatever is lovely, whatever is of good repute, if there is anything worthy of praise, let your mind dwell on these things.*

2 Timothy 2:22 *Run away from anything that gives you the evil thoughts that young men often have, but stay close to anything that makes you want to do right. Have faith and love, and enjoy the companionship of those who love the Lord and have pure hearts.*

2 Timothy 3:6 *For among them are those who enter into households and captivate weak women weighed down with sins, led on by various impulses.*

2 Peter 2:7 *And if He rescued righteous Lot, oppressed by the sensual conduct of unprincipled men (for by what he saw and heard that righteous man, while living among them, felt his righteous soul tormented day after day with their lawless deeds), then the Lord knows how to rescue the godly from temptation, and to keep the unrighteous under punishment for the day of judgment.*

Some things, some people, and\or some situations influence us to hate, some to love, some to lust, some to anger, some to peace, some to discipline, some to laziness. Each person reacts differently to each influence, but each person is influenced by everything. When a person sees a forest or a movie or hears an orchestra or a heavy metal concert, it all influences for good or bad. It may only exert a mild influence on a person, but it exerts an influence. If we are to present ourselves to God as an acceptable sacrifice, we must get a handle on the influences of our lives.

HOW TO GET A HANDLE ON THE INFLUENCES OF MY LIFE...

1. Realize that influences are judged by their effects or results

This means that it is NOT possible to tell whether a particular thing is a good or a bad thing just by deciding whether I want to do it or whether a lot of other people are doing it. This means that something is not necessarily a good thing just because it makes me feel good in the present (drugs, alcohol, affairs, cheating). All influences must be judged by their ultimate effect or result in my life.

What are the evil, unrighteous, harmful, or foolish things that I am doing or want to do?

1.

2.

3.

4.

5.

6.

7.

8.

9.

10.

It is sometimes more helpful to let someone close to you who you can trust fill out the things that are foolish, unrighteous, harmful, or evil.

What are the influences that are encouraging these activities?

Put the influences next to the activity.

Put down an influence even if it is not the total cause of the activity.

2. Learn what produces negative results in your life

No matter what the feeling or the seeming gain of certain activities – if it produces the evil, selfish, foolish, or sinful traits the Bible condemns – then you know that it is a negative influence. What does the Bible describe as evil outcomes:

Romans 1:29-31 What makes me think, act, and speak with...

Greed, Malice, Envy, Murderous Intentions, Strife, Deceit, Gossip, Slander, Hatred Toward God, Insolence, Arrogance, Boastful, Evil, Disobedience to Parents, Disloyalty, Unloving Spirit, a lack of mercy

Galatians 5:19 What makes me think, speak, and act more...

Immoral, Impure, Sensual, Idolatrous, Superstitious, Vengeful, Spiteful, Jealous, Explosive with Anger, Argumentative, Disagreeable, Factious, Envious, Drunken, Carousing

1 Peter 4:3 What makes me think, speak, and act more...
Unnecessarily sexual, Unable to contain my bodily appetites, Intoxicated and out of control, Carousing, Wild (Party-goer), Accepting of False Religions

3. Learn what influences you to be more pleasing to God

In the same way that we can only tell whether something is unfavorable by what it pushes us toward in the long run, so we can only tell about the good influences in our lives by examining what the activities make us do in the long run.

What are the wise, helpful, or righteous activities that I am doing?

1.

2.

3.

4.

5.

6

7.

8.

9.

10.

This is another case in which is best to let someone else point out your positive points.

What are the influences that tend to push me toward these positive things? Put them next to the activity.

Galatians 5:22,23 What things make me think, speak, and act more... Loving, **Joyful**, Peaceful, Patient, Kind, Meek, Faithful, Self-Controlled

Philippians 4:8 What things make me think, speak, and act more... Truthful, Mannered, Respectful, Humble, Righteous, Pure, Pleasant, Lovely, Wise, Excellent, Filled with Praise

4. Ruthlessly substitute the positive for the negative.

Jesus said, "If your right hand causes you to stumble cut it off and throw it from you. If your right eye causes you to stumble cut it out and throw if from you." Matthew 5:29,30

We will never conquer our temptations and bad habits until we are willing to substitute a positive action, idea, or practice for a negative one. It is not enough to just say that we will no longer do the negative. If we do not put a positive practice in its place, then a vacuum is created and we will go back to thinking about the evil influence or action.

Colossians 3:5,12 *Therefore consider the members of your earthly body as dead to immorality, impurity, passion, evil desire, and greed, which amounts to idolatry... And so, as those who have been chosen of God, holy and beloved, put on a heart of compassion, kindness, humility, gentleness, and patience...*

Write down the influences that you think are keeping you tied to this type of behavior.

1.

2.

3.

4.

5.

6.

7.

8.

9.

10.

Turning Anger

into a Controlled Soul

Ephesians 4:22-27

Turning Anger into a Controlled Soul Ephesians 4:22-27

Many are convinced that anger is not a problem in their life. In fact, many use it as a tool or a weapon to get their way. I have a friend who is wonderful except for the hand grenade of anger she carries with her. She rarely uses it but is always ready to throw an anger bomb. She is a wonderful mother, a wonderful wife, and an exemplar employee. She regularly gets praise for how she acts in each of these roles. Ninety-nine percent of the time she goes above and beyond the call of duty in each of these roles. But about every month to month-and-a-half she verbally vomits on the people in her life. She is angry and she lets the people around her have it. She had been known to hold her colleagues at work hostage to her rants. She has blown through a number of husbands who at some point have refused to put up with this withering barrage of emotional venom. Her children tip toe around wondering if Mt. Mom is about to blow. She looks at the ninety-nine percent of her life that is wonderful and righteous and loving and says to herself that she is a really good person. Everyone else who has ever experienced the volcano of anger walks with nervousness around her. She cannot understand why people have a problem with her. She only occasionally gets mad. To her the wonderful work that she does most of the time more than makes up for her rants. But that is not how others see it. They give her a wide berth. They make excuses why she is not included in their close circle of friends. There is a reason she has not married again.

Truths about Anger

1. Anger is a reaction to life as it has just presented itself to you. Anger is an emotion and that means it is a reaction to something in your life. Your soul has been tuned by the experiences and choices of the past to react with anger to whatever just happened. Not everyone reacts this way to what just happened, but you do. Your anger is like the sound that comes from guitar strings that have been strummed. Your anger is like a rash that bubbles up when you brush up against poison oak. Your anger is an allergic rash you have developed to life when it presents itself to you in this way. Now the important thing to realize is that you can change this reaction in a number of ways. It is up to you to choose to change this reaction so you do not disqualify yourself from levels of success and opportunities that can be yours. Let's talk about a few ways of adjusting your reaction.

A. Avoid the situation, people, circumstances, or pressures that produced the rash of anger.

What are three typical times when you get angry?

1.

2.

3.

How can you avoid the situation, people, or circumstances that trigger your anger?

1.

2.

3.

If you usually get angry every time you are around Jim or Sally for more than a few minutes, then what can you do to avoid being around them for that long?

If you usually get angry when you go to a party at a certain place or with certain people, then what can you do to avoid parties at those places or with those people?

If you usually get angry when you are under time pressure or financial pressure, then what can you do to plan better and avoid the time or money pressure?

B. Change the situation or problem in some way so that it doesn't trigger this angry reaction.

What are three typical times when you get angry?

1.

2.

3.

What ways can you change the situation, problem, people, or pressures to not get angry?

1.

2.

3.

If you usually get angry every time you are around Jim or Sally for more than a few minutes, then what can you add to your time with them (people, circumstances, rewards, punishments, information) so that you will not get angry if you are around them for a while?

If you usually get angry when you go to a party at a certain place or with certain people, then what can you add (people, circumstances, rewards, punishments, information) to those parties, those places, or being with those people so you will not get angry?

If you usually get angry when you are under time pressure or financial pressure, then what can you add to your basic time management and/or financial management to avoid getting angry?

C. React in a different way to this problem

What are three typical times when you get angry?

1.

2.

3.

What ways can you react to the situation, problem, people, or pressures in a different way other than anger? You will be creating a completely different reactive pattern here. Realize here that you know people who do not react with anger in exactly the same situation that produces anger in you. What are they doing? How do they channel their reaction down a different path than you are channeling yours? Be very specific here. I could do this or say this or reward myself in this particular way if I didn't get angry or I could laugh it off in this way, etc.

1.

2.

3.

Let me suggest a few:

Laughter

Taking notes

Push-ups

Some form of physical movement or exercise

Quoting Scripture – out loud or under your breath

Psychoanalyzing the other person or yourself

Pinching yourself

Deep breaths

Examining your expectations for the trigger

If you usually get angry every time you are around Jim or Sally for more than a few minutes, then what different reactions could you develop so that you will not get angry if you are around them for a while?

If you usually get angry when you go to a party at a certain place or with certain people, then what different reactions could you develop so you will not get angry?

If you usually get angry when you are under time pressure or financial pressure, then what different reactions could you develop to avoid getting angry?

2. Anger is emotional fuel for making changes. God has given us the emotion of anger in order to fuel changes that are needed in our life, our relationships, and in our world. But anger in its raw form is useless. In fact, anger in its raw form is destructive. It must be controlled and refined to become useful. Anger is like a fire and there is a difference between your drapes catching fire and having a fire in the fire place. One is controlled and the other is not. Anger is like an explosion and there is a difference between an explosion and an engine. An engine is a harnessed explosion that produces useable energy. Much of your anger in the past has been an explosion. It has been you screaming, "I WANT CHANGE!!!" But you couldn't control this energy nor the change it brought. Your anger caused change but not positive, directed, helpful change. If you are angry, then it is a signal that change is needed. Either the change is on your end, from others, or in the world at large. The presence of anger is a signal that change is needed.

Understand what you are trying to do is turn your soul and body into an engine that will use the explosion of anger to fuel the changes that are needed for you and others to win. You will learn to contain the explosion of your anger and turn it into energy to keep you moving toward your goals. Yes, at times you will feel like your insides are exploding with the anger you feel for the change that is needed. As you contain this energy, use it to work toward the dreams, goals, and people God has given you.

If you are angry, then God is sending you a signal that change is needed. Where is the change needed: in you, in your place, in your circumstances, in your response, in others, in the systems, organizations, institutions, and governments around you? Remember we live in a sinful world where people are allowed to be selfish, hurtful, oppressive, and destructive. Therefore your anger is a reaction to something that doesn't seem right to you. It may be that you are the one who is not right. It may be others who are not right. It may be the systems, organizations, institutions, and governments that are not right. But change is needed for harmony to be achieved.

Your anger is signaling a need for change; you must find the changes and make them.

Where is the change needed?

What changes would cause you to not be angry anymore?

The more specific and doable the changes you list the better

In you? –

What changes?

In your place? –

What changes?

In your circumstances? -

What changes?

In your response? -

What changes?

In others? –

What changes?

In your relationships? –

What changes?

Organizations –

What changes?

Institutions around you? –

What changes?

Government officials or systems? –

What changes?

3. Anger in its raw form is destructive and must be refined to be utilized. The raw energy of anger must be refined if it is to become a constructive force in our lives. Anger in its raw form blames, criticizes, mopes, attacks, plots, schemes. You can't put raw anger into your life and expect it not to damage relationships, work, finances, future plans, etc. The presence of anger is a signal that change is needed in some part of your life.

Let's take a look at your anger. We need to come to grips with the various forms of our anger in their destructive forms and understand how long anger has been a part of our lives and our family background. Work through this check list of expressions of anger and pray the prayer of confession and repentance at the end.

Check	Involvement with Anger, Violence, or Murder	Who Practiced? You / Relative
	Outbursts of anger	
	Rage	
	Wrath – seething when in that person's presence	
	Burning resentment – inability to escape thinking about what they did and what you would like to do back	
	Malice – delighting in planning harm to the person; doing harm to them	
	Violence against others – often to get your own way	
	Assault – physical, sexual, financial	
	Murder – mental/emotional, racial, abortion, physical, spiritual, sexual	

Take the time to ask God for forgiveness for your destructive anger and the way it has messed with your life and your family's life. Admit that anger is wrong. Turn over this area of change, expectations, and power to God. The following is a suggested prayer in confessing your anger.

A Prayer of Confession

This is a suggested prayer of confession. Take each person and/or situation where you have demonstrated an unhealthy self-focus and admit to God that you were wrong. This is not a magical formula; it is a suggested prayer. But the ideas of confession, repentance, renunciation, cleansing, and transfer are powerful.. It is your sincerity and honesty before God that is important.

1. Confession and Repentance (1 John 1:9: 2 Timothy 2:24)

Lord Jesus, I agree with you that anger is wrong. I turn away from it and ask that all the forgiveness that is in your death on Calvary be applied to my sin in this area. You say in your Word that anger, rage and hatred is wrong for you say "The anger of man does not achieve the righteousness of God." I realize that only in your power and through your direction can I successfully turn away from this sin.

2. Renunciation (2 Corinthians 4:4)

I repudiate, reject, and renounce any ground, place, or power I gave to Satan in my life through my involvement in anger. I give to the Lord Jesus Christ all power over this area of my life. I willingly surrender this area to the Lord Jesus Christ and the Holy Spirit.

3. Cleansing and Expulsion (1 John 1:9; Ephesians 4:27)

I cancel any contract I may have made with Satan through anger. I ask you, Lord Jesus, to cleanse me of any and all unrighteousness (including demons and demonic strongholds) because you say in your Word in 1 John 1:9 that "if we confess our sins He is faithful and just to forgive us our sins and to cleanse us of all unrighteousness."

4. Transfer of Ownership and Infusion of the Spirit of Truth (2 Corinthians 10:3-5; Colossians 1:27,28; Ephesians 5:18)

I right now transfer ownership of change and expectations in my life to the Lord Jesus Christ. I choose to take every thought regarding anger, change, expectations captive to Christ (2 Corinthians 10:3-5) and allow Him full lordship in this area. I ask you, Lord Jesus, that you would fill this area of my life with the Holy Spirit of truth, so that I would be wise, thankful, and able to see your plan in this area in the future. Thank you, Lord Jesus, for dying on the Cross for me. I choose to cooperate with you in developing calm flexibility so that the process you began in me when I first trusted in You can continue. (Philippians 1:6). I realize that you want to display through me the character qualities of the Lord Jesus (Colossians 1:27,28; Galatians 2:20).

In the Name and for the Glory of the Lord Jesus Christ,

Amen

In order for a prayer of confession to be maximally effective in breaking very powerful satanic strongholds and influence, it is best if this prayer is prayed out loud with a mature Christian brother or sister who is watching you pray and is praying with and for you.

As we move further into helping you move past destructive anger, let's take a look at repairing some of the damage of your destructive anger. There are two aspects of your anger of the past that need to be dealt. **First,** much of the way you have expressed your anger has been destructive. You have exploded all over people and organizations in damaging ways. Even some of the beneficial changes that you tried to accomplish were done in damaging ways. You have exploded at people, on people, and devalued them in order to get the change you wanted. Those need to be admitted as the wrong way of going about life. You will find that some of the people who were closest to you bore the brunt of your angry explosions. They didn't deserve it and your anger may have destroyed friendships and opportunities.

Who do you need to apologize to about your explosions of anger? Start by looking at those closest to you: Family, Friends, Colleagues, and Neighbors.

1.

2.

3.

4.

5.

6.

7.

8.

9.

10.

Second, some of your anger is just your being selfish and wanting everything to go your way. It is the anger that comes from, "If I were God, then people would drive differently, do what I want immediately, do things my way, not be offensive, stop doing what I find irritating." Temper tantrum anger because things didn't go your way is childish. You will need to grow up and let that kind of anger go. Realize that you are not God and we are all very glad. There is energy in selfish anger, but it is the energy to grow up and adapt to the real world.

What are the things that regularly tick you off but are really just you wanting everything to go the way you want with little consideration for others?

1.

2.

3.

4.

5.

6.

7.

8.

9.

10.

Confess these to the Lord as selfish. Let Him know that you want to grow past anger over these selfish things.

A **third** aspect of anger that you will need to work through is the anger of others directed at you or affecting you. Many of you may have borne the brunt of other people's anger. Their anger may have left you demeaned, devalued, and damaged in some way. It can be very helpful to admit that what they did was wrong and undeserved. There is something freeing when you can admit to God out loud in prayer that the anger you experienced was wrong. Confession is a way of admitting the truth. Confession is also asking God to come and fill in the places where the destructiveness of others has left huge holes in our life.

Who has been angry at you or demeaned you, devalued you, or damaged you through their outbursts of rage?

1.

2.

3.

4.

5.

6

7.

8.

9.

10.

Pray a prayer of confession to God that these people's anger was wrong and an inappropriate way to change you or their situation.

Ask this next question to complete the understanding of the other person's anger. Was there anything that you did that caused these people to unleash their anger on you? Look at the list of people from above and write down what they were thinking that justified their being angry at you.

1.

2.

3.

4.

5.

6.

7.

8.

9

10.

Who are the people and organizations you have been angry at?

1.

2.

3.

4.

5.

6.

7.

8.

9.

10.

11.

12.

13.

14.

15.

16.

17.

18.

19.

20.

4. Anger is about expectations. There is a difference between how we all react to wishes and expectations. When what I wish or dream doesn't happen, we are disappointed or whimsical; but when an expectation doesn't happen, we get angry. Anger is a reaction to something that we told ourselves was supposed to happen but did not. If we are going to get a handle on our anger, then we are going to have to get a handle on our expectations. How fast do our desires harden into expectations? Why do some desires never harden into expectations and some do almost immediately? How long will we give ourselves, God, and others to bring about an expectation? How do I make my expectations goals instead of expectations? In order to conquer anger, we have to work with your responsibility in the accomplishment of your dreams, goals, and expectations.

What do you find yourself getting angry about most often?

What did you expect to happen other than what did happen?

Anger   **Expectation**

1.

2.

3.

4.

5.

What can you do so that next time you get closer to achieving your expectation or so you don't react in anger to not achieving it?

<u>What change can you do to totally transform the situation?</u>

1.

2.

3.

4.

5.

6.

7.

8.

9.

10.

The longest section on anger in Scripture is Ephesians 4:26-32. Read through this Scripture ten times slowly and let its truths sink into your mind. Write it out by hand at least once.

BE ANGRY, AND yet DO NOT SIN; do not let the sun go down on your anger, and do not give the devil an opportunity. He who steals must steal no longer; but rather he must labor, performing with his own hands what is good, so that he will have something to share with one who has need... Let no unwholesome word proceed from your mouth, but only such a word as is good for edification according to the need of the moment, so that it will give grace to those who hear. Do not grieve the Holy Spirit of God, by whom you were sealed for the day of redemption. Let all bitterness and wrath and anger and clamor and slander be put away from you, along with all malice. Be kind to one another, tenderhearted, forgiving each other, just as God in Christ also has forgiven you.

Take each sentence or phrase of Scripture and picture what it would look like if you were doing what this verse says. Actually picture yourself going through the day living out the truths of this Scripture.

I would speak like this…

I would act like this…

I would be thinking this…

I would react in this way to so and so…

I would take time to…

I wouldn't do…

I would help…

I would want to…

On Our Way to Meekness: A controlled soul

MEEKNESS is about being flexible and adaptable to the way life unfolds. God may have a different goal or different time table than we do. We may not see our expectations realized immediately or even in years, but we need to stay true to God's purposes and His goals. Meekness is Strength Under Control. Would people describe you as a controlled person; as a person who is flexible and adaptable to change? The most successful people are people who remain flexible, adaptable, and controlled under pressure even as they pursue their dreams and goals with power. Meekness involves discerning when our rights, privileges, possessions, and even schedules are in the way of God's plan. The easiest way to begin discovering this violation is by looking at anger. Meekness is the ability to yield at a moment's notice to the superior plan of God without getting angry. There are times when we should not yield—when the person around us means us harm or would seek to have us do that which is immoral. God will constantly ask us to yield to Him so that the joy of meekness can be ours.

Note: **Once** you have realized what God is doing and why it is important, then predetermine how you will respond the next time you are faced with this situation and remain flexible and alert for God's purpose.

In prayer tell God that you want to yield your expectations, your desires, and your possession to Him. Picture the next time you will be faced with the choice of being angry and instead see yourself yielding the right, possession, expectation, and desire. Tell God that you want Him to have it for His bigger purpose.

Learn to make reasonable requests of those around you and of God.

Write out reasonable requests which would change your situations so you wouldn't be angry. You may need a separate sheet of paper to fully develop these requests.

To God

To Yourself

To Others

Learn to set limits for yourself; when to go further would cause anger.

I usually get angry when…

      I am tired

      I am around certain people

      I am caught off guard

      I am sick

      I am being told what to do

      I am doing something I think is beneath me

      I don't like what I am doing

      I am in a hurry

      I am under financial pressure

      I am not getting along with my spouse

      I am disrespected

      I am pressured to do something

Eight Steps to Overcome Anger

Write this eight-step process on a card and carry it with you. This week when you become angry, use the following eight steps in dealing with anger:

1. Be aware of it. Admit you are reacting in anger to something in your life

> Say or think "I am angry/"

2. Answer the question:

> What do I have an unrealistic expectation about?

3. Accept responsibility for the *fact* of your anger. I am responsible for my reaction to my life.

> I can choose not to be angry. Because I have chosen to be angry...

4. Decide who or what is going to have control of your life.

> You can allow your anger to control you or with the Holy Spirit, you can choose to control your anger.

5. Identify the source and cause of your anger.

> Am I hurt? Am I frustrated?
>
> Do I have unmet or blocked goals and desires?
>
> Am I selfish? Am I afraid?

6. Choose your response.

> Am I going to spend my energy being angry or invest it?

7. What change is this anger giving me the energy to attempt?

1.

2.

3.

4.

5.

8. What act of love can I perform that will deny me the pity party my "selfishness" wants to have because I have been hurt?

Turning

Occult Involvement

into

Worship of God Alone

Matthew 4:4; Exodus 20:3-6

Turning Occult Involvement into Worship of God Alone Matthew 4:4; Exodus 20:3-6

It is true that there are false gods and false Christ's in the world. Everyone is free to choose whatever god they want to serve. Whatever god we choose to worship and serve will bring consequences into our lives. The God of the Bible, both Old and New Testament, is the supreme God who created the world and asks for full allegiance. He offers freedom from our sins and a home in heaven, but He will not embrace being one of a group of gods that a person worships. Many people have been led astray into the worship of false god's. If one is going to become serious about experiencing freedom in Christ, then one must deal with God's demands for exclusive worship. One of the most serious actions a person can take is to cut ties with other gods and begin to worship exclusively and fully the God of the Bible. The following are the steps that move one from observer of God to a true worshipper and citizen of heaven.

STEP 1: BECOMING A FULLY COMMITTED CHRISTIAN

The one antidote to the problems associated with past occult involvement is a complete surrender to the Lord Jesus Christ. If you have never asked Jesus Christ to save you from your sins and run your life, then ask Him right now. While the other steps to getting rid of occult bondage can be done, they are of little value without a fully surrendered life. If you are a Christian who has been backsliding or not fully committed, then it is time to rededicate your life to God. The only barrier that the Devil respects is the blood of the Lord Jesus Christ. You must be fully dedicated to Christ Jesus—no half-hearted measures.

Prayer to fully commit your life to Jesus Christ:

Dear Lord Jesus,

I need you. I realize that I am a sinner. I want you to be my Savior and come and run my life. Come and make me the kind of person you want me to be. Thank you for dying on the Cross for my sins. I realize that I am giving you the right to run my life.

In the Name of the Lord Jesus Christ,

Amen

Step 2: CLEANING OUT YOUR HOUSE

The following is a suggested list of items that may be in your home which can give the Devil an advantage in your life. The scriptural method for destroying these objects is by smashing and/or burning (Exodus 32:19,20; Judges 6:25-28). This renders the objects unusable and therefore unwanted by another. It is recommended to pray after the objects have been destroyed and state the command: "Satan and the demons are no longer welcome here and must leave in the name of the Lord Jesus Christ. Whatever ground or place may have been given to Satan through my possession or use of this object is canceled and given completely over to the Lord Jesus Christ to be occupied by the Holy Spirit."

Occult Statues

There are a number of statues which are not idols in the classic sense but have strong occult ties and overtones. These would include the following statues:

Wizards, Trolls, Demons, Bats, Serpents, Witches, Evil Castles, Ghosts and Goblins, Gremlins. All types of tapestries which glorify evil or satanic practices

All these types of statues should be removed from the home of the Christians. It does not matter whether the statue is a cute version of a satanic creature; it should be destroyed and removed. One of the greatest deceptions is that cute things cannot be harmful. Remember, your home should be a place of safety and refuge, not a battle ground. Your home should be safe for the weakest Christian to find shelter and comfort.

Occult Objects

The secular market place is filled with objects that have occult significance. These objects induct the unwary into Satan's realm and have no business in the home of the Christian. It is a false hope to believe that a Bible on the shelf counteracts all occult objects.

Crystals (used for channeling power), Ouija Boards, Tarot Cards, Pyramids, Pentagrams, Good Luck Charms, Amulets, Egyptian Worship Symbols, Talisman, Astrology Charts

All these objects are used to call upon Satan and his demonic hordes, and they should not be treated lightly. Christians should not use, glamorize, or promote the occult in any way.

Occult Jewelry

There is an abundance of jewelry with devils, dragons, bats, skulls, and other strongly occultic themes which should be destroyed. There is no reason why a Christian should wear the marks of death and satanic bondage. Christians should proclaim in every area of life that they belong to the Lord Jesus Christ and have chosen to walk in the kingdom of light. There are certain types of jewelry which are not occult in their form but which have been made for or used in mystical or demonic religions (this would include some American Indian jewelry). This type of jewelry should not be owned, worn, and should be destroyed.

Occult Books

There are many different types of occult books from the New Age literature to the satanic bible which should be removed from the house. These books detail practices of evil. They can also act as place of operation for oppressive evil spirits. The list grows longer every month. If you believe a book, magazine, or article is satanic or evil, don't have it in your home. It doesn't matter that it is valuable. Get rid of it.

Pornography

This would include all types of pornography from soft core (airbrushed pictures of scantily-clad women) to hard core (graphic depictions of sexual relations). Pornography also includes written material which contains no pictures but describes sexuality or sexual acts in a seductive, alluring, immoral, or degenerate fashion.

Cult Books

There are many books produced which are not overtly occult or demonic but pervert the truth of God and the faith once delivered to the saints. Unless God has called you to a specific ministry of dealing with these groups, these books should not be in your home.

Music

There is a great debate about various types of music and its impact on Christians. Any music which arouses immoral, violent, or sinful desires is to be discarded. Any music which details satanic practices or offers praise to Satan or demons is to be discarded. Any music which captivates one's mind so that little room is left for meditation on the Scriptures and the Lord Jesus Christ is to be discarded. The following categories of music are examples of types of music which should be destroyed. This list should not be taken as a complete list. Each individual must examine every piece of music to which he/she listens.

Occult Practices

The most obvious area to receive demonic attachment or demonic oppression is involvement in the occult. Each area of involvement in the occult should be brought before the Lord in confession, repentance, and renunciation. In the next section there is a list of occult, cultic, and perversion practices. Check off the areas you have personally been involved The Christians needs to cut themselves off spiritually from these practices and enter into full adoption in the family of God.

STEP #3: SEVERING OCCUTIC TIES

In order to fully be free of the attachments and oppression of the past occult practices and associations, it is often the most helpful to go back through all of your past involvements and confess these to the Lord Jesus Christ. Each one of these needs to be handled individually as a confession item. Do not seek to bunch these together in a blanket confession. If it becomes hard to pray a prayer of confession over any item, then take the time to work through, with your mentor, your involvement in that practice. Then have your mentor pray for you about this issue and then press in again to agree with God about this issue. Keep pushing on.

Check	Involvement in the Occult	Level of Involvement (Mild, Moderate, Heavy)
	Occult practices	
	Astrology	
	Witchcraft	
	White Magic	
	Black Magic	
	Séances	
	Magical Role Playing Games	
	ESP	
	Clairvoyance	
	Medium	
	Spiritism	
	Second Sight	

Check	Involvement in the Occult	Level of Involvement (Mild, Moderate, Heavy)
	Mind Reading	
	Fortune Telling	
	Palm Reading	
	Tea Leaf Reading	
	Crystal Ball	
	Tarot Cards	
	Horoscopes	
	Reincarnation	
	Metaphysic Healings	
	Deep Hypnosis	
	Curses, Hexes, Vexes	
	Spells	
	Charms	
	Oaths; Death, Blood, etc	
	Voodoo	
	Santeria	

Check	Involvement in the Occult	Level of Involvement (Mild, Moderate, Heavy)
	Levitation	
	Psychometry	
	Automatic Writing	
	Channeling	
	Numerology	
	Occultic Literature	
	Psychic Phenomena	
	Crystals	
	Pyramid Power	
	Pacts with the Devil	
	Sacrifices (ritual and actual)	
	Bride of Satan	
	Para psychology	
	Religious Yoga	
	Transcendental Meditation	
	Spirit Guides	

Check	Involvement in the Occult	Level of Involvement (Mild, Moderate, Heavy)
	Ascended Masters	
	Estactic Utterance	
	Prophecy	
	Religious or Spiritual Acupuncture	
	Conversation with Spirits	
	Black Mass	
	Mind Control	
	Death Magic	
	Free Masonry	
	Poltergeists	
	Psychic abilities	
	Queen of Darkness; Queen of black witches	
	Spiritist prophecy, soothsaying	
	Spiritistic magic	

Check	Involvement in the Occult	Level of Involvement (Mild, Moderate, Heavy)
	Transfiguration, Translocation, Materialization, Apports, Deports,	
	Symbols of Occult Peace: Egyptian Fertility, Pentagram, etc.	
	Vampires	
	Weleda Medicines	
	Speaking in Trance	
	Satan Worship	
	Table Lifting	

Work through the confession prayer for each of the areas you practiced a spiritual offense. There can be significant benefit to actually taking the time to agree with God that each of these involvements was against his plan and destructive to your future. Many people are in a hurry to offer a blanket prayer. Don't do that. Take the time to pray through each of these areas of sin with your mentor. The suggested prayer walks you through the essential elements of a cleansing confession time. It may take some time, but it will be worth it. Declaring your agreement with God's viewpoint on elements in your life is very helpful.

Check	Other Religions	Level of Involvement (Mild, Moderate, Heavy)
	Hinduism	
	Buddhism	
	Islam	
	Rosicrusianism	
	Hare Krishna	
	Masons	
	Satanism	
	Science of the Mind	
	Bahaism	
	Jean Dixon	
	Scientology	
	Mormonism	
	Jehovah Witness	
	Unification Church	
	Unity	
	Meher Baba	

Check	Other Religions	Level of Involvement (Mild, Moderate, Heavy)
	Edgar Cayce	
	Masons	
	EST	
	Scientology	
	Silva Mind Control	
	Eckanar	

Work through the confession prayer for each of the areas you practiced a spiritual offense. There can be significant benefit to actually taking the time to agree with God that each of these involvements was against his plan and destructive to your future. Many people are in a hurry to offer a blanket prayer. Don't do that. Take the time to pray through each of these areas of sin with your mentor. The suggested prayer walks you through the essential elements of a cleansing confession time. It may take some time but it will be worth it. Declaring your agreement with God's viewpoint on elements in your life is very helpful.

Check	Perversions of the 10 Commandments	Level of Involvement (Mild, Moderate, Heavy)
	Worship of Other Gods	
	Misrepresenting God through idols or creating and worship of other gods through Idols	
	Swearing, Cursing and Living against God's nature and name	
	Failure to acknowledge God regularly	
	Rebellion against God – given authorities who were trying to direct, protect, provide and comfort you	
	Murder, Torture, Violence, Outbursts of Anger	

Check	Perversions of the 10 Commandments	Level of Involvement (Mild, Moderate, Heavy)
	Sexual Infidelity, Sexual Abuse, Sexual harm	
	Stealing	
	Fraud, Lying, Deception for personal profit or to escape personal pain	
	Scheming to take others relationships, possessions or work	

Work through the confession prayer for each of the areas you practiced a spiritual offense. There can be significant benefit to actually taking the time to agree with God that each of these involvements was against his plan and destructive to your future. Many people are in a hurry to offer a blanket prayer. Don't do that. Take the time to pray through each of these areas of sin with your mentor. The suggested prayer walks you through the essential elements of a cleansing confession time. It may take some time but it will be worth it. Declaring your agreement with God's viewpoint on elements in your life is very helpful

A Prayer of Confession

This is a suggested prayer of confession. You do not have to use these exact words. But these ideas of confession, repentance, renunciation, cleansing, and transfer should be present. This is not a magical formula; it is a suggested prayer. It is your sincerity and honesty before God that is important.

1. Confession and Repentance (1 John 1:9: 2 Timothy 2:24)

Lord Jesus, I agree with you that _____ is wrong. I turn away from it and ask that all the forgiveness that is in your death on Calvary be applied to my sin in this area. You say in your Word that _____ is wrong for you say _____. I realize that only in your power and energy and through your direction can I successfully turn away from this sin.

2. Renunciation (2 Corinthians 4:4)

I repudiate, reject, and renounce any ground, place, or power I gave to Satan in my life through my involvement in _____. I give to the Lord Jesus Christ all power over this area of my life. I willingly surrender this area to the Lord Jesus Christ and the Holy Spirit.

3. Cleansing and Expulsion (1 John 1:9; Ephesians 4:27)

I cancel any contract I may have made with Satan through _____. I ask you, Lord Jesus, to cleanse me of any and all unrighteousness (including demons and demonic strongholds) because you say in your Word in 1 John 1:9 that "if we confess our sins He is faithful and just to forgive us our sins and to cleanse us of all unrighteousness."

4. Transfer of Ownership and Infusion of the Spirit of Truth (2 Corinthians 10:3-5; Colossians 1:27,28; Ephesians 5:18)

I right now transfer ownership of _____ in my life to the Lord Jesus Christ. I choose to take every thought regarding _____ captive to Christ (2 Corinthians 10:3-5) and allow Him full lordship in this area. I ask you, Lord Jesus, that you would fill this area of my life with the Holy Spirit of truth, so that I would be wise, thankful, and able to see your plan in this area in the future. Thank you, Lord Jesus, for dying on the Cross for me. I choose to cooperate with you in _____ area of my life so that the process you began in me when I first trusted in You can continue. (Philippians. 1:6). I realize that you want to display through me the character qualities of the Lord Jesus (Colossians 1:27,28; Galatians 2:20).

In the Name and for the Glory of the Lord Jesus Christ,

Amen

In order for a prayer of confession to be maximally effective in breaking very powerful satanic strongholds and influence, it is best if this prayer is prayed out loud with a mature Christian brother or sister who is watching you pray and is praying with and for you.

Step #4: Cleaning out your spiritual experiences

It is important to examine all areas and experiences of our lives, even those which we have always assumed have come from God. We need to make sure that the Devil has not sought to deceive us by appearing as an angel of light (2 Corinthians 11:14). Any and all valid supernatural experiences and abilities need to be celebrated. Any experiences or abilities that do not find their source in God the Holy Spirit must be rejected and renounced!

Have you had a spiritual or supernatural experience? Please describe.

1.

2.

3.

Have you in the past or do you now have any psychic abilities? Please describe.

1.

2.

3.

Have you ever had any charismatic Christian experiences? Please describe.

1.

2.

3.

Since the time of your supernatural experience have you had a greater or lesser ability to resist temptation? Please describe.

Do you have any of the following spiritual gifts: healing, tongues, prophecy, interpretation of tongues, words of wisdom, words of knowledge, miracles, or discernment of spirits? Please describe.

1.

2.

3.

Did you evidence any of these abilities before you were a Christian? Please describe.

1.

2.

3.

Have you ever had a supernatural healing? Please describe.

1.

2.

3.

If you have received a supernatural experience, gift, ability, or guide, have you had a greater or lesser love for the Bible? Please describe.

1.

2.

3.

Have you ever had your supernatural gift, ability, experience, or guide tested? Please describe.

1.

2.

3.

Testing Your Spiritual Experiences

There are three biblical tests that can be run on a supernatural experience or event.

1. The Fruit of the gift: Matthew 7:15-20

What is the person' life like who has the gift or is offering the gift? If their life is continually impure, then the gift may be impure.

2. The Content of the gift: 1 Corinthians 12:1-3

What are they proclaiming? All kinds of people are purporting to be giving messages from God but does this message line up with the Bible and the truth in Jesus Christ?

3. The Source of the gift: 1 John 4:1-4

Who is the author of the gift? It is possible to test whether the source of the gift is from the Holy Spirit of God. Ask it directly if Jesus Christ is the Lord of All (1 Corinthians 12:3). Ask it if Jesus the Christ has come in the Flesh to be the Savior of the World (1 John 4:1).

If you have received a supernatural experience, gift, ability, or guide from the Holy Spirit, it should constantly move you to display the Fruit of the Spirit. If instead you are constantly plagued by thoughts that are the opposite of the fruit of the Holy Spirit, this is a clue that the gift, experience, ability, or guide is not from the Lord Jesus Christ.

Please circle those that apply and then describe:

Love vs. hatred, unforgiveness, resentment, bitterness, jealousy, murder

Joy vs. depression, despair, discouragement, disillusionment, suicide

Peace vs. anxiety, tension, worry, confusion, restlessness, breakdown

Longsuffering vs. impatience, selfishness, disharmony, anger, wrath, violence

Kindness vs. harshness, selfishness, cruelty, argumentative, possessive

Goodness vs. filthy thoughts, pornography, evil imaginations, immorality

Meekness vs. pride, ego, self-exaltation, dissension, unteachable, materialistic

Faith vs. doubt, hesitation, anxiety, negative perspective, agnosticism, atheism

Self-Control vs. addictions, no discipline, slander, gossip, compulsive behavior

Renounce anything that does not produce the fruit of the Holy Spirit in your life. No matter how good it makes you feel or how much money comes to you through it.

Step #5: Cleaning Out Your Relationships

If you maintain friendships with those who are still involved in the occult, then this could be a source of defeat for you. Their ties to the occult can and do cause you to be vulnerable to the attacks and oppression of the Enemy. Some of your old friends want to drag you back into the life and practices of your past. You need to sever that relationship in most cases. On the other hand, anyone who is actually moving toward Christ should be encouraged to continue their spiritual journey.

Make a list of your current friends. Make a note if they are involved in the occult.

1.

2.

3.

4.

5.

6.

7.

8.

9.

10.

Make a list of any friends from your past who were in the occult.

1.

2.

3.

4.

5

6.

7.

8.

9.

10.

Step #6: Cleaning Out Your Wisdom

We live life on the basis of sayings we have learned, experiences that we have had, and things that we have been told. Whenever we come to a crucial decision or just live our lives day to day, we draw upon this knowledge and it helps us make our decisions. Unfortunately, much of what we draw on is not God's wisdom. It is possible for us to have an entire bank of information that is the opposite of God's wisdom. If this material was the result of occult influences, involvement, and/or oppression, it needs to be examined and replaced by godly thought patterns.

Make a list of saying that you have always believed were truisms:

1.

2.

3.

4.

5.

6.

7.

8.

9.

10.

Describe in detail five experiences that you feel have made a significant impact on your life:

1.

2.

3.

4.

5.

Make a list of ten people who have changed the course of your life for good or evil with a brief explanation of why they are significant:

1.

2.

3.

4.

5.

6.

7.

8.

9.

10.

Step #7: Dedicating Your House

Ask your pastor to come to your house and pray in each room after it has been cleansed of any material that should not be there. He may anoint each door post with oil as a symbol of the Holy Spirit's presence. Make sure that he and you give your house to the Lord Jesus Christ for His purposes.

Describe what has taken place since your pastor has come to your house and dedicated the place where you are living.

Step #8: Dedicating Your Soul

Make an appointment with your pastor to pray a prayer of dedication to God and His service. It is important that you do this with a pastor or church leader as God works through the church to accomplish His purposes. This means that you want to pray a prayer that dedicates your mind and all its mental power and subconscious activities to the Lord Jesus Christ, asking that you dedicate your will to the Lord Jesus Christ so that He might show you clearly what His choices are and that you would sense His desire to do them. The final area involved in dedicating your soul is the area of your emotions. Give the Lord Jesus Christ your emotions. Place them under His care and tell Him that you are willing to have them be subservient to your mind. Ask Him to share with you the perspectives that will allow your emotions to easily bend to His will.

Describe what has happened since you have prayed this prayer of dedication with your pastor.

Step #9: Dedicating Your Relationships

Find another dedicated Christian who will pray with you as you give God all your relationships. You will allow Jesus Christ to pick your friendships. You will move toward Him and allow Him to eliminate those who really do not have a desire to serve Him. Remember that it is not your job to advise Jesus who He should retain or eliminate. Your job is to follow after Him and see who else is going that way.

What has happened since you have prayed this prayer dedicating your relationships to the Lord Jesus Christ?

Step #10: Dedicating Yourself

It is important that each day we rededicate ourselves to the Lord Jesus Christ by keeping short accounts of our sins and by giving ourselves over to His will. This process of being a living sacrifice is not a one-time action but rather a daily occurrence. Let the Lord know each morning when you get out of bed that you are ready to live for Him. Let Him know that you want the Holy Spirit to fill you so that you will be instantly obedient to His will.

Dear Heavenly Father,

I come in the name of Your Son, the Lord Jesus Christ. I want to thank you for all the gifts that You have given me today. I am excited to live for you today. Make me alert to your promptings and your special appointments as I go through the day.

Amen.

Turning Transference

into

Spiritual Freedom

Matthew 4:4; Exodus 20:3-6

Turning Transference into Spiritual Freedom

The definition of transference is all those ways which demonic spirits might use to transfer in or around a person without the person being specifically involved in a sin in the past. The demonic spirits would then seek to cause the person to sin or to move at their impulse so that they can have a greater measure of control. There are three areas that could produce a transference problem: ancestral sins, victimization, and curses.

Ancestral Sins: Any of the doorways which have been discussed are potential doorways to what are called familiar spirits in that they are familiar with your family and the type of sin that your family is most tempted by. Members of each generation must recognize that they are the inheritors of the good and bad from the previous generations. Each individual must deal with his/her tendencies and susceptibility to sin in certain areas. This would include family and cultural patterns of sin and immorality which are accepted by the individual without even evaluating its morality.

Victimization: This is any behavior which is abusive behavior which is perpetrated upon the individual. This behavior is oppressive and is usually designed to establish or retain control over the person. It is not beneficial but instead oppressive and destructive. It would include physical abuse, sexual abuse, emotional abuse, mental abuse, spiritual abuse, and even financial abuse.

Curses: Another area of transference is curses placed on a person, family, or object. These need to be canceled or destroyed and the person, family, or object redeemed. These curses might include familiar spirits, oaths, (blood, death, other), hexes, vows, curses, vexes, spells, charms, amulets, psychic abilities taken out against or on the person, family, or object.

Transference problems can be dealt with in four steps: **information, confession, repentance, infusion of truth.** These four steps may have to be repeated a number of times as ever deeper layers are uncovered in this area of transference. Often a first pass through this material is done by the individual and then a second pass with educated probing with a trusted mentor. Then a third pass through this material may be made with the help of prayer warriors or safe family members. A final pass may be made through this material with those who have the gifts of discernment of spirits and their spiritual eyes on these parts of a person's past. In the area of transference in the confession step, you are not taking personal responsibility for the sinful acts of your parents; but you are agreeing with God that those actions were wrong and damaging. It is powerful when you acknowledge basic morality and orient yourself to what God says about immoral actions. It breaks the hold of that person, demon, or sin in your life and allows you to walk away from spiritual influences connected with those actions.

Information

Step #1: Confession of Generational Sin

In order to fully be free of the attachments and oppression of the past occult associations, it is often the most helpful to go back through all of your past involvements and confess these to the Lord Jesus Christ. Each one of these needs to be handled individually as a confession item. Do not seek to bunch these together in a blanket confession. If it becomes hard to pray a prayer of confession over any them, keep pushing on.

Your Parents' Spiritual and Moral History

An important issue to cover with people who are experiencing spiritual oppression is how involved their parents were in the occult and/or immorality. The following list can be very informative about the family history of these areas. In this list the person is answering about their family, not themselves. Put a check mark by what was done and who did it. Many people have wondered about some of the practices listed which they don't know anything about. If you do not know what something is, then just skip it and move on. We will assume that if you do not know about it, your family did not practice it.

Check	Involvement in Pride	Who practiced?
	Pride – Self-Focus	
	Arrogance- Superiority	
	Bigotry - Prejudice	
	Criticism – Cynical	
	Unteachable spirit	
	Lack of Self-Acceptance	

Check	Involvement in Rebellion	Who practiced?
	Unrighteous rebellion	
	Lack of submission	
	Rebellious Attitude – negative attitude toward authority	
	Lack of teamwork	
	Lack of servant's heart	

Check	Involvement with Lust and Adultery	Who practiced?
	Pornography	
	Mental adultery	
	Transvestitism	
	Immoral conduct: indecent exposure; voyeurism; masturbation; sexual harassment	
	Premarital sexual encounters	
	Adultery	
	Prostitution	

Check	Involvement with Lust and Adultery	Who practiced?
	Homosexual episodes	
	Incest	
	Bestiality	
	Satanic – ritual sexuality	

Check	Involvement with Anger, Violence, and Murder	Who practiced?
	Outbursts of anger	
	Rage	
	Wrath	
	Burning resentment	
	Malice	
	Violence against others	
	Assault	
	Murder	

Check	Involvement with Bitterness, Revenge, and Forgiveness	Who practiced?
	Bitterness	
	Revenge	
	Lack of forgiveness	
	Rejoicing in harm of others	
	Refusal to move on	

Check	Involvement in the Occult	Who practiced?
	Occult practices	
	Astrology	
	Witchcraft	
	White Magic	
	Black Magic	
	Séances	
	Magical role-playing games	
	ESP	

Check	Involvement in the Occult	Who practiced?
	Clairvoyance	
	Medium	
	Spiritism	
	Second Sight	
	Mind Reading	
	Fortune Telling	
	Palm Reading	
	Tea Leaf Reading	
	Crystal Ball	
	Tarot Cards	
	Horoscopes	
	Reincarnation	
	Metaphysic Healings	
	Deep Hypnosis	
	Curses, Hexes, Vexes	
	Spells	

Check	Involvement in the Occult	Who practiced?
	Charms	
	Oaths; Death, Blood, etc	
	Voodoo	
	Santeria	
	Levitation	
	Psychometry	
	Automatic Writing	
	Channeling	
	Numerology	
	Astral Projection	
	Occultic Literature	
	Psychic Phenomena	
	Crystals	
	Pyramid Power	
	Pacts with the Devil	
	Sacrifices (ritual and actual)	

Check	Involvement in the Occult	Who practiced?
	Bride of Satan	
	Para psychology	
	Religious Yoga	
	Transcendental Meditation	
	Spirit Guides	
	Ascended Masters	
	Ecstatic Utterance	
	Prophecy	
	Religious Acupuncture	
	Conversation with spirits	
	Black Mass	
	Mind Control	
	Death Magic	
	Free Masonry	
	Poltergeists	
	Psychic abilities	

Check	Involvement in the Occult	Who practiced?
	Queen of Darkness; Queen of black witches	
	Satan Worship	
	Table Lifting	
	Speaking in trance	
	Spiritist prophecy, soothsaying	
	Spiritistic magic	
	Transfiguration, Translocation, Materialization, Apports, Deports	
	Symbols of Occultic Peace: Egyptian Fertility, Pentagram, etc.	
	Vampires	
	Weleda Medicines	

Check	Violations of the Ten Commandments	Who Practiced? (Mild, Moderate, Severe)
	Worship of other gods; practicing other religions	
	Misrepresenting God through idols or creating and worship of other gods through idols	
	Swearing, cursing, and living against God's nature and name	
	Failure to acknowledge God regularly; laziness and an unwillingness to do the good works that you could do	
	Rebellion against God – given authorities who were trying to direct, protect, provide, and comfort you	
	Murder, torture, violence for personal ends	
	Sexual activity outside of marriage	
	Stealing	
	Fraud, lying, deception for personal profit or to escape personal pain	
	Scheming to take others relationships, possessions, or work	

Check	Other Religions	Who Practiced? (Mild, Moderate, Severe)
	Hinduism	
	Buddhism	
	Islam	
	Rosicrusianism	
	Hare Krishna	
	Masons	
	Satanism	
	Science of the Mind	
	Bahaism	
	Jean Dixon	
	Scientology	
	Mormonism	
	Jehovah Witness	
	Unification Church	
	Unity	

Check	Other Religions	Who Practiced? (Mild, Moderate, Severe)
	Meher Baba	
	Edgar Cayce	
	Masons	
	EST	
	Scientology	
	Silva Mind Control	
	Eckanar	

Using the above list from the last category, go through sins again and note your family's involvement. Acknowledge in prayer it was evil and against God's laws and desire. Even though you may not have committed them personally, confess that these sins were wrong in the sight of God. Complete the confession work sheet as an interested party, not the perpetrator of any sins that your family may have committed.

A Prayer of Confession

This is a suggested prayer of confession. You do not have to use these exact words. But these ideas of confession, repentance, renunciation, cleansing, and transfer should be present. This is not a magical formula; it is a suggested prayer. It is your sincerity and honesty before God that is important.

1. Confession and Repentance (1 John 1:9: 2 Timothy 2:24)

Lord Jesus, I agree with You that _____ is wrong. I turn away from it and ask that all the forgiveness that is in your death on Calvary be applied to my sin in this area. You say in your Word that _____ is wrong for you say _____. I realize that only in your power and energy and through your direction can I successfully turn away from this sin.

2. Renunciation (2 Corinthians 4:4)

I repudiate, reject, and renounce any ground, place, or power I gave to Satan in my life through my involvement in _____. I give to the Lord Jesus Christ all power over this area of my life. I willingly surrender this area to the Lord Jesus Christ and the Holy Spirit.

3. Cleansing and Expulsion (1 John 1:9; Ephesians 4:27)

I cancel any contract I may have made with Satan through _____. I ask you, Lord Jesus, to cleanse me of any and all unrighteousness (including demons and demonic strongholds) because you say in your Word in 1 John 1:9 that "if we confess our sins He is faithful and just to forgive us our sins and to cleanse us of all unrighteousness."

4. Transfer of Ownership and Infusion of the Spirit of Truth (2 Corinthians 10:3-5; Colossians 1:27,28; Ephesians 5:18)

I right now transfer ownership of _____ in my life to the Lord Jesus Christ. I choose to take every thought regarding _____ captive to Christ (2 Corinthians 10:3-5) and allow Him full lordship in this area. I ask you, Lord Jesus, that you would fill this area of my life with the Holy Spirit of truth, so that I would be wise, thankful, and able to see your plan in this area in the future. Thank you, Lord Jesus, for dying on the Cross for me. I choose to cooperate with you in _____ area of my life so that the process you began in me when I first trusted in You can continue. (Philippians 1:6). I realize that you want to display through me the character qualities of the Lord Jesus (Colossians 1:27,28; Galatians 2:20).

In the Name and for the Glory of the Lord Jesus Christ,

Amen

In order for a prayer of confession to be maximally effective in breaking very powerful satanic strongholds and influence, it is best if this prayer is prayed out loud with a mature Christian brother or sister who is watching you pray and is praying with and for you.

Victimization

The second area in which a person must deal with possible transference problems is the area of victimization. This is destructive behavior which is perpetrated upon the individual. This behavior is oppressive and is usually designed to pleasure the perpetrator or establish or retain control over the person. It is not beneficial but instead oppressive and destructive behavior done to the victim. These behaviors would include physical abuse, sexual abuse, emotional abuse, mental abuse, spiritual abuse, and even financial abuse.

It is important that someone who has been abused be able to morally condemn the attack and their attacker and seek justice without going beyond into hatred, personal vengeance, and/or becoming a perpetrator themselves. The abused individual can and should be able to morally condemn the action, move into forgiveness, and put it behind them emotionally even as they may seek to make sure that others do not suffer the same victimization that they suffered.

Make a list of any forms of abuse that you suffered. Demonic oppression has been known to begin after a brutalization, abuse, and/or ritualistic deathbed ceremonies. It is possible that your very understanding of the brutalization keeps you in bondage to wicked spirits. Jesus said, "You shall know the truth and the truth shall make you free." (John 8:32)

Physical Abuse

Incident	People Involved	Action Applied
1.		
2.		
3.		
4.		
5.		
6.		
7.		
8.		
9.		
10.		

Mental Abuse

Incident	People Involved	Action Applied
1.		
2.		
3.		
4.		
5.		
6.		
7.		
8.		
9.		
10.		

Sexual Abuse

Incident	People Involved	Action Applied
1.		
2.		
3.		
4.		
5.		
6.		
7.		
8.		
9.		
10.		

Spiritual Abuse

Incident	People Involved	Action Applied
1.		
2.		
3.		
4.		
5.		
6.		
7.		
8.		
9.		
10.		

MOURNING YOUR LOSSES, YOUR WOUNDS, YOUR PAIN

People who move to the depths of Christian spirituality have learned to mourn. When a person has been victimized, it becomes crucial that they process the pain of that event and are able to work through what has happened to them. Jesus said clearly that the person who was able to mourn their pain and even their guilt were the blessed ones, not the ones who kept their pain, wounds, and guilt secret. In order to receive the blessings of mourning we must do it much more deeply than most want to go. It is very powerful to process your pain by getting it out of your soul through writing, talking, and even praying it out.

Jesus was right when he said that we cannot be truly blessed in this sinful world without practicing mourning. Remember even He mourned the physical death of Lazarus in John 11. We live in a sinful world in which terrible things happen to us because other people are allowed to make selfish choices. These losses, wounds, and pain can cripple us if we do not process them. To mourn means to process these significant negative events in our life. It could be the death of a loved one. It could be a sexual molestation or rape. It could be a divorce. It could be abandonment or loneliness. It could be the loss of a job.

I have two friends who each wasted over twenty years of their lives in alcohol and drug addictions. Both of them have been delivered from that slavery and have gone on to advanced degrees and now are helping people who are lost in the same addictions they struggled with. They both told me that there are essentially two things that make an addict. One, you must be in the presence of the substance that is addictive to you. Two, you must have a wound that you are trying to self-medicate so you don't have to feel its pain any more. Both of these men separately told me that when they try and help an addict, they must help the person bring out the wound or all treatment will fail. It is the unprocessed wound that keeps them addicted to whatever will make that pain go away.

We must know how to mourn to survive this sinful world. There will be pain, wounds, and loss as we live out our lives. We must be able to process the difficulties of those times. Make an appointment with a counselor, a trusted friend, a pastor, and/or a safe person and talk through some or all of the most painful episodes in your life. This may take time. Process your pain. You must express your pain, your feelings, and your wounds outside your soul.

Dealing with Curses, Hexes, Vexes, Oaths, Spells, and Charms

In the spirit world it is possible to place lingering negative influences on people, families, objects, and groups. These come under the title of curses, hexes, vexes, oaths, spells, and charms. At times in order to enjoy the fullest freedom in Christ, it is very helpful to cancel out any of these lingering negative spiritual influences. These can be canceled through the work of Christ Jesus on the cross. This process of canceling the impact of any of these elements goes through a threefold process: **Uncovering, Canceling, Resisting.**

Step #1: Uncovering

As we make progress in our spiritual life, we can become aware of a block or attachment that is keeping us from going forward. One of the things that may be holding us back is a curse, hex, vex, oath, spell, or charm that has been placed upon us, our family, an object we own, or something of this nature. When we become aware of something like this, we should cancel it out in the Name of the Lord Jesus Christ.

Is it necessary to begin searching through our family history or past to see if a curse has been placed on us? No!!! But when we become aware of a spiritual influence that is lingering in our life after we have become Christians and we are impeded in some aspect of our spiritual life, we may want to see if there has been any of these spiritual anchors attached to our life. The process of canceling them out again goes back to the finished work of Christ on the cross and the cleansing that comes from Him. Pray the suggested prayer below and work through the three steps of uncovering, canceling, and resisting.

Dear Heavenly Father,

I come in the name of the Lord Jesus Christ to ask that you would show me the ways that Satan or his demons are influencing or attempting to influence my life through curses, hexes, vexes, oaths, spells, and charms. I am thankful, Heavenly Father, that you want me to know the truth so that I can move into the freedom of the Lord Jesus Christ.

In the Name of the Lord Jesus Christ, Amen

Step #2: Canceling

Any power, place, or influence that may have been placed in your life that is designed to keep you from God's best can be canceled by being in Christ. Any agreement that was made is canceled when a person enters into the adoption arrangement of becoming a Christian. God adopts them into His forever family. The Devil still wants to enforce old agreements and blockages, but you have been set free in Christ. Embrace the freedom that is in Christ and declare the truth that in Christ any old covenants, charms, powers, and boundaries are canceled. In the Lord Jesus Christ you have been given the power and the grace to be anything and everything He wants you to be. You now serve the Almighty God, the King of Kings, who has adopted you and wants you to enjoy life with Him.

Heavenly Father,

I come in the name of the Lord Jesus Christ who is my Savior and my Lord. I thank you that you know what I cannot know. I thank you that you are all powerful and have chosen to set your love upon me in Christ. I ask you, Heavenly Father, to cut off, cancel, and nullify any curses, hexes, vexes, charms, oaths, and spells which have been placed against me or said over me or in any other way have influenced my life. I ask this so that I might live to the complete glory of God in every area of my life. I desire to be, by the grace of God my Savior, a trophy for all to see of the power of Jesus Christ.

In the Name of the Lord Jesus Christ,

Amen

Step #3: Resisting the Effects

If you were under some type of curse or hex, it was only there because you gave it power by letting it be an obstacle. In the power of Christ you are free from its power, but you must prove that it does not have power over you. Remember, that even after you say these prayers, the same spiritual influence will try and probe your life to see if you will still give in to the same lies, fear, and blockages as before. You must resist and do what Christ is calling you to do.

Heavenly Father,

I realize, Heavenly Father, that you have allowed the sins of the fathers to penetrate to the third and fourth generations of those who hate you. I confess the following areas have been problems for my family in the past._____. I freely admit that the sins and lawlessness of my ancestors will make me a special target for those same areas of sinfulness. I ask you to show me the areas in my life where I must make special plans to resist the Devil and his demons. I ask you to work specifically in my life to bring me to the place where I will be able to powerfully resist the activity of the wicked spirits. I desire that you build through my life a godly heritage. I realize that you multiply your grace to the generations that will follow me if I will successfully depend upon you to defeat the tactics and schemes of the Devil.

I ask you, Heavenly Father, to show me the ways to resist the work of the Enemy in my life and to frustrate his plans for me. I desire to live for you, Lord Jesus, and to display your power, wisdom, and grace to a watching world. I am incapable in myself of resisting the schemes of Satan, but in Christ I am able to live a new life for I am a new creation in Him. Show me how I must fortify my life in order to counteract the specific curses, hexes, vexes, spells, charms, and oaths that have been set up against me. Show me how I must grow in order to overcome my sinful tendencies. Bathe my mind with the scriptural truth that I need to think your thoughts after you.

Heavenly Father, reveal to me any demonic strongholds, any demonically-induced mental patterns or logic, emotional feeling or guilt, physical traits, characteristics, or objects that are the result of a curse, hex, vex, oath, spell, or charm.

In the Name of the Lord Jesus Christ,

Amen

Conclusion

Conclusion: Surveying the growth you have made

Thank you for working your way through the various exercises in this book. You have taken steps many people are unwilling to take in your search for freedom, blessing, and closeness with God. Many people have gone through the exercises in this book a number of times. Let me suggest at least four different journeys through this material.

Level 1: Go through this with a mentor, pastor, friend, or counselor. This is the level that you have most likely gone through this material the first time. This mentor-driven journey allows you to work through the material with a prayer partner and someone to keep you accountable to keep going through the material. There will be times when you do not want to keep going. Facing our past and building a different future is difficult, but essential. My hope is that you have been on this journey with a mentor, pastor, friend, or counselor. If you have not gone through this material with a trusted advisor, then go through the material in this way. Let them direct you through the material. Let them hear what has happened in your past and pray with you and help you walk out of the struggles, patterns, and bondages of the past.

Look at how much you have worked through and give praise to God for your progress. You may notice that you still have more to go but give thanks and praise for what has been accomplished.

Check if Completed	Exploring your past and your programming	Comments
Check if Completed	Involvement in pride	Comments
Check if Completed	Involvement in rebellion	Comments
Check if Completed	Involvement with lust and adultery	Comments
Check if Completed	Involvement with anger, violence, and murder	Comments

Check if Completed	Involvement with bitterness, revenge, and forgiveness	Comments
Check if Completed	Involvement in the occult	Comments
Check if Completed	Violations of the Ten Commandments	Comments
Check if Completed	Involvement with other religions	Comments
Check if Completed	Involvement with transference: ancestral sin, victimization, curses	Comments

Level 2: Go through the various areas and categories of sin and righteousness a second time on your own. Look at the categories and pray through them. "Which areas do I still need to work on, Lord?" "Lord Jesus, which categories should I start working on now?" "Lord, are their particular exercises or projects that you want me to do?" As you go through the material on your own, you can do the same exercises again that you did before or you can do new exercises that you did not do the last time in a particular section. Let God guide you or just go through the whole book again from beginning to end. Pray the prayers again. Allow this individual work to be a new experience. It can be very helpful to have people praying for you as you go through this material and have someone or a group hear what is happening. A small group may form around individuals who want to go through the material individually and then report to the group what is happening. Let me say again, I recommend going through the material individually as the second time you have tackled this material, not the first. As you pray, number the various sections based upon the order that you sense God wants you to go back through these areas.

Priority	Exploring your past and your programming	Comments
Priority	Involvement in pride	Comments
Priority	Involvement in rebellion	Comments
Priority	Involvement with lust and adultery	Comments
Priority	Involvement with anger, violence, and murder	Comments
Priority	Involvement with bitterness, revenge, and forgiveness	Comments
Priority	Involvement in the occult	Comments

Priority	Violations of the Ten Commandments	Comments
Priority	Involvement with other religions	Comments
Priority	Involvement with transference: ancestral sin, victimization, curses	Comments

Level 3: Have people with spiritual gifts of prayer, wisdom, discernment, and knowledge pray for you about any lingering strongholds and areas of oppression that may still exist. After they pray, they should be able to write down what they sense from the Lord as they pray for you. This can be very helpful to pinpoint any areas that need further work. They may tell you (or write down) that they sense issues with anger or rebellion that have not been sufficiently dealt with and that need attention. You would then go to that section of the book and work through some more of the projects and exercises in that section.

I have seen people make significant progress on being free from negative spiritual influences when they are spiritually directed to specific areas of their life that they may not even realize are areas of oppression and darkness. The basic categories of this book are a spiritual template to pray for others who are still having difficulty enjoying the whole of Christ's victory over darkness. Your church should have a prayer team with people who can pray for others. Ask them to pray for you in the categories of this book to see if there are still areas of your life that the Devil is hiding in. I have included a detailed list of the categories of this book as a template for the prayer team. Make a copy of this template and put you name on the top and ask people to pray for you in these areas. "Is there still more work needed in any of these areas?"

Many people want to go to this third level of work with these sins and areas of righteousness. But skipping over the diligence needed to complete the first two levels is essential. I do not recommend skipping the crucial step that is given in Joshua, "Every place the soul of your foot shall tread, I will give it to you as a possession." We must walk through the whole of our life and face what is there, clean up the mess, bring order, and apply the victory that is in Christ to that area. We need to demonstrate that we really want to be free in Christ, that we are really willing to be courageous. In most cases we do not need to do this third level of work in a person's life. The first and/or second level is sufficient. I will give you two templates covering the contents of this book: A survey and a more detailed template.

Priority	Exploring your past and your programming	Comments
Priority	Involvement in pride	Comments
Priority	Involvement in rebellion	Comments
Priority	Involvement with lust and adultery	Comments
Priority	Involvement with anger, violence, and murder	Comments
Priority	Involvement with bitterness, revenge, and forgiveness	Comments
Priority	Involvement in the occult	Comments
Priority	Violations of the Ten Commandments	Comments
Priority	Involvement with other religions	Comments
Priority	Involvement with transference: Ancestral sin, victimization, curses	Comments

Prayer Warrior Template for Becoming Courageous:

Facing Your Past – Building Your Future

Name of Person:

Check	Involvement in Pride	Comments
	Pride – Self-Focus	
	Arrogance- Superiority	
	Bigotry - Prejudice	
	Criticism – Cynical	
	Unteachable spirit	
	Lack of self-acceptance	

Check	Involvement in Rebellion	Comments
	Unrighteous rebellion	
	Lack of submission	
	Rebellious attitude – negative attitude toward authority	
	Lack of teamwork	
	Lack of servant's heart	

Check	Involvement with Lust and Adultery	Comments
	Pornography	
	Mental adultery	
	Transvestitism	
	Immoral Conduct: indecent exposure; voyeurism; masturbation; sexual harassment	
	Premarital sexual encounters	
	Adultery	

Check	Involvement with Lust and Adultery	Comments
	Prostitution	
	Homosexual episodes	
	Incest	
	Bestiality	
	Satanic – ritual sexuality	

Check	Involvement with Anger, Violence, and Murder	Comments
	Outbursts of anger	
	Rage	
	Wrath	
	Burning resentment	
	Malice	
	Violence against others	
	Assault	
	Murder	

Check	Involvement with Bitterness, Revenge, and Forgiveness	Comments
	Bitterness	
	Revenge	
	Lack of forgiveness	
	Rejoicing in harm of others	
	Refusal to move on	

Check	Involvement in the Occult	Comments
	Occult practices	
	Astrology	
	Witchcraft	
	White Magic	
	Black Magic	
	Séances	
	Magical Role-playing Games	
	ESP	

Check	Involvement in the Occult	Comments
	Clairvoyance	
	Medium	
	Spiritism	
	Second Sight	
	Mind Reading	
	Fortune Telling	
	Palm Reading	
	Tea Leaf Reading	
	Crystal Ball	
	Tarot Cards	
	Horoscopes	
	Reincarnation	
	Metaphysic Healings	
	Deep Hypnosis	
	Curses, Hexes, Vexes	
	Spells	

Check	Involvement in the Occult	Comments
	Charms	
	Oaths; Death, Blood, etc	
	Voodoo	
	Santeria	
	Levitation	
	Psychometry	
	Automatic Writing	
	Channeling	
	Numerology	
	Astral Projection	
	Occult Literature	
	Psychic Phenomena	
	Crystals	
	Pyramid Power	
	Pacts with the Devil	

Check	Involvement in the Occult	Comments
	Sacrifices (ritual and actual)	
	Bride of Satan	
	Para psychology	
	Religious Yoga	
	Transcendental Meditation	
	Spirit Guides	
	Ascended Masters	
	Ecstatic Utterance	
	False Prophecy	
	Religious Acupuncture	
	Conversation with Spirits	
	Black Mass	
	Mind Control	
	Death Magic	
	Free Masonry	
	Poltergeists	

Check	Involvement in the Occult	Comments
	Psychic abilities	
	Queen of Darkness; Queen of Black Witches	
	Satan Worship	
	Table Lifting	
	Speaking in Trance	
	Spiritist prophecy, soothsaying	
	Spiritistic magic	
	Transfiguration, Translocation, Materialization, Apports, Deports,	
	Symbols of Occultic Peace: Egyptian Fertility, Pentagram, etc.	
	Vampires	
	Weleda Medicines	

Check	Violations of the Ten Commandments	Comments
	Worship of other gods; practicing other religions	
	Misrepresenting God through idols or creating and worship of other gods through idols	
	Swearing, cursing and Lliving against God's nature and name	
	Failure to acknowledge God regularly. Laziness and an unwillingness to do the good works that you could do	
	Rebellion against God – given authorities who were trying to direct, protect, provide, and comfort you	
	Murder, torture, violence for personal ends	
	Sexual activity outside of marriage	
	Stealing – defrauding – devaluing	
	Fraud, lLying, deception for personal profit or to escape personal pain	
	Scheming to take others relationships, possessions, or work	

Check	Other Religions	Comments
	Hinduism	
	Buddhism	
	Islam	
	Rosicrusianism	
	Hare Krishna	
	Masons	
	Satanism	
	Science of the Mind	
	Baha'i	
	Jean Dixon	
	Scientology	
	Mormonism	
	Jehovah Witness	
	Unification Church	
	Unity	
	Meher Baba	

Check	Other Religions	Comments
	Edgar Cayce	
	Masons	
	EST	
	Scientology	
	Silva Mind Control	
	Eckanar	

Check	Form of Transference: Ancestral Sin	Comments
	Involvement in pride	
	Involvement in rebellion	
	Involvement with lust and adultery	
	Involvement with anger, violence, and murder	
	Involvement with bitterness, revenge, and forgiveness	
	Involvement in the occult	
	Involvement in the transference: ancestral sins, victimization, curses, hexes, vexes, spells, charms	

Check	Form of Transference: Victimization	Comments
	Physical abuse	
	Mental/emotional abuse	
	Sexual abuse	
	Spiritual abuse	

Check	Form of Transference: Curse, Hex, Vex, Talisman, Spells, Charm	Comments
	Curse	
	Hex	
	Vex	
	Talisman	
	Spells	
	Charm	

Level 4: Become a mentor, counselor, or friend for someone else going through the material. Many times when you are helping someone else understand a concept and praying for them, you see the truth in a new light. Loving someone else enough to help them is often a wonderful way of growing ourselves. It does not matter that you may only be a few steps ahead of the people you are helping. It matters that you are willing to help and that this other person respects you enough to ask for you as their mentor, sponsor, or trusted friend. Helping others gives you a new perspective on what you are battling yourself.

Let me leave you with this prayer that you can pray as you strive to please the Lord Jesus Christ in all you do. Your journey into and with Christ is worth it. Do not grow weary but keep pressing on for the high calling of knowing Jesus Christ our Lord.

Dear Heavenly Father,

Thank you for loving me enough to give your only begotten Son to become a human, live a perfect life, and then sacrifice His perfect life to pay for the sins of the whole world. I realize that you, Lord Jesus, are my only hope for heaven and power and ability I have to live a righteous, spiritual life before you. Thank you again for all the spiritual blessings that you give me each day. I pray that I will have eyes to see them and use them. I pray that I may grow in the grace and knowledge of the Lord Jesus Christ every day and display the fruit of the Holy Spirit in my life so that you get great glory.

In the Name of the Lord Jesus Christ,

Amen

About the Author

Gil Stieglitz is an internationally recognized author, speaker, catalyst, counselor, professor, pastor, and leadership consultant. He is Executive Pastor of Adventure Christian Church, a mega-church of 4,000 in Roseville, California. He teaches at Christian universities and graduate schools in practical theology (Biola, William Jessup, Western Seminary). He is the President of Principles to Live By, an organization committed to teaching God's principles in a life-giving way. He sits on several boards, including Thriving Churches International, a ministry extension of Bayside Church, and Courage Worldwide, an organization that builds homes throughout the world to rescue children forced into sexual slavery. He has been a denominational executive for fifteen years with the Evangelical Free Church of America and was the senior pastor of a vibrant church in southern California for seventeen years.

He has a Master's Degree in Biblical Exposition and a Doctorate in Christian Leadership with a special emphasis in Spiritual Warfare.

Other Resources by Gil Stieglitz

Available in various formats from books to e-books, Kindle, audio, and podcasts. Check out www.ptlb.com for more information.

Breaking Satanic Bondage

Deep Happiness: The 8 Secrets

Developing a Christian Worldview

God's Radical Plan for Husbands

God's Radical Plan for Wives

Going Deep In Prayer: 40 Days of In-Depth Prayer

Leading a Thriving Ministry: 10 Indispensable Leadership Skills

Marital Intelligence: A Foolproof Guide for Saving and Strengthening Marriage

Mission Possible: Winning the Battle Over Temptation

Spiritual Disciplines of a C.H.R.I.S.T.I.A.N.: Intensive Training in Christian Spirituality

They Laughed When I Wrote Another Book About Prayer ...Then They Read It: How to Make Prayer Work

Touching the Face of God: 40 Days of Adoring God

Why There Has to Be a Hell

If you would be interested in having Dr. Stieglitz

speak to your group, you can contact him

through the website

www.ptlb.com

CPSIA information can be obtained
at www.ICGtesting.com
Printed in the USA
FSOW02n0009050815
9392FS

9 780983 860259